No Regrets

Timothy C. Pruitt, MBA

No Regrets

Timothy C. Pruitt

2025 All rights reserved.

This publication may not be reproduced, stored in an electronic system, or transmitted in any form or by any means, electronic, mechanical, photocopy, recording, or otherwise, without proper credit to the author. Brief quotations may be used without permission.

Scripture quotations are from the King James Version unless otherwise noted.

ISBN 978-1-961482-23-4

Table of Contents

Foreword i
Author's Preface ii
The Characters and the Setting iv
The Journey Begins 1
    Answering the Call 2
    A Sure Foundation 10
Matters of the Heart 16
    Beware of the Lone Wolf 17
    The Evolution of Vision 25
    Connecting (your community) 32
    Being Consumed with Passion 40
    The Capacity for Mercy 48
    The Trajectory of Responsibility 54
    Fitly Framed 61
    Connecting (the lost) 69
    What They Need 75
    The Call from the Hungry 83
    The Cultural Leader 91
Practical Matters 97
    Developing a Long-term Plan 98
    Developing a First-year Plan 107
    Building Teams 114
    The Cement of Administration 122
    Panic 132
    Define Your Funnel 141
    The Juggler 150
    Creating a Financial Foundation 162
    Developing Leaders 170

Table of Contents

Finishing the Journey 177

    Creating a Launch Plan 178

    The Launch Location 185

    The Launch Service 194

    Transition 203

    The Juggler - Reprise 210

    Everything 217

    A Legacy of Service 226

    A Vision for Reproduction 236

Appendix 1 - Scorecard 243

Appendix 2 - Program Template 251

About the Author 258

Foreword

For many, there is a wide gap between the inspiration of a God-given calling and the activation of that call. Through a beautifully woven narrative, Tim Pruitt skillfully instructs and inspires those called to the work of church planting, offering both practical insight and spiritual encouragement.

Rev. Joshua B. Carson
Senior Pastor / Calvary Tabernacle
Indianapolis IN

Church Planting is one of the hardest yet, most rewarding, challenges of Apostolic ministry. My family of four started a mission work almost 700 miles away from our home. Just like foreign missionaries, we had to learn a different culture, a different religious mindset, and a new style of the English language! Oh, what I would have given to have a book like this to help guide us through the process. I highly recommend this well written work as a remarkable resource for any missionary family!

Rev. Steve Williams
Church Planter
Martinsville VA

Author's Preface

Those accepting the challenge and, with it, the calling, to plant a church commit themselves to a tremendous task. But few know the experiences that entails. Those aspiring to take this noble challenge embark bravely in what is mostly a mystery. For others who have not received such a calling but are interested, nonetheless, in the stories that those brave souls tell, it is an exploration of something entirely new and different. This book helps unveil that shroud of mystery.

The format is a series of short narratives that describe typical episodes in the lives of those who plant churches. Most of the stories are the voice of the pastor. Some are told from the perspective of the pastor's wife or the children.

It is not a biography of a particular family. It is a narrative that can be told by many. Their stories are typical. The narratives are based on testimonials of those who have planted churches. The intent is to honestly, and sometimes with raw expression, describe two things. The first is to describe what church planters do. The second is to describe what happens in a church planter's heart.

This book is intended to prepare and encourage those who will plant churches. My prayer for you is that this story, in some measure, will inspire you to continue, that it will strengthen your commitment to your calling, and that you will willingly identify with this story that can also be yours.

It is also intended for those interested in learning of the experiences of those that plant churches. This story, filled with determination, fulfillment and spiritual bravery, will amaze you. Your admiration for those who have persevered in their pursuit will most certainly grow.

Author's Preface

These are typical stories, but their order is notional. Sequence will vary from one planted church to another. There has been some grouping, and in some cases, one story may reference something said in another. Many of the stories interwoven in these narratives are real stories from actual church planters. As much as possible, each story is a distinct narrative, standing on its own.

This book is a companion book to a previous book, *Effective Christianity: Managing Life's Projects*. At the end of each story are associated references from that book.

I have great appreciation for the North American Missions Division of the United Pentecostal Church International. Their One-Button Planning materials were a tremendous inspiration and influence on these narratives. Many of the topics in this book are a direct reflection of their anointed and experienced presentations.

I would also like to thank the following for their help in reviewing and contributing ideas for this book:

Gary Walls	Charlene and David Dugas
Doris Golder	Peggy and Larry Jenkins
Jolie Kinney	Beth and Tim Massengale
Richard E. French, Jr	Jane and Steve Williams
Neil and Sonia Mack	

Great appreciation is due to my pastor, Rev. Joshua B. Carson, for his input and support, and for the assistance of the Creative Team at Calvary Tabernacle in the cover design for this book.

Finally, I thank my lovely wife, Rita, for your continual encouragement and, most of all, your companionship.

Timothy C. Pruitt

The Characters and the Setting

These narratives center around a pastor and his family. They are the Martinez family. There are four members of the family, and thus, four primary characters in these narratives. Each of those characters is described below:

THE PARENTS

The parents are the main characters in most of the narratives. Most of the conversations take place between them.

<u>The Pastor</u>: Married for 20 years, Edwin Martinez is the pastor and a father of two teenage children. He is of average income, and the primary, but not only, wage earner in the family. Edwin has a sister. His parents are saved, but they are not in the ministry. He does his best to be a good and appreciative husband to his wife, Ava. Being a good father to two teenage children has its challenges, but his love for them has never been stronger. Edwin is a minister who has supported a local church and pastor. He has a great relationship with his current pastor, and now feels a calling to plant a church in another city.

<u>The Pastor's wife</u>: Having been married to the pastor, Edwin, for 20 years, Ava Martinez is the mother of the previously-mentioned two teenage children. Though focused on her children, she has done what she can to help supplement her husband's income. Ava has a brother. Like her husband, her parents are saved, but they are not in the ministry. Ava is devoted to her husband and her children.

The Characters and the Setting

Through every adolescent struggle, she has provided wise guidance and direction to them. She too has been active in supporting their local church, and is well-liked and respected in that local church. As the narratives will tell, Ava shares the calling in their lives to plant a church in another city.

THE CHILDREN

Though most of the conversations are between the parents, the children are not insignificant characters. The experiences described in these narratives are a combined team effort of the family. Each family member is important.

The Pastor's Son: Daniel Martinez, now a young man, is a typical teenager, who enjoys being active with his friends. He participates in activities at church and at school. Daniel has deeply personal friends at both church and school. At this stage in his life, he has no ministerial or leadership aspirations. He's not yet thinking about a family, but does picture himself as having a job that would support a family financially. For now, Daniel wants to enjoy the life he has. He has typical quarrels with his younger sister, but those quarrels are of little consequence. Daniel loves his family (including his sister), respects both parents, and values their commitment to the ministry.

The Pastor's Daughter: Like her older brother, Mia Martinez is active with her friends at church and at school. She is a young lady whose friendships are deep, and maybe more emotionally so than those of her brother, Daniel. That is especially true for her friends at their local church. Mia dreams of being a wonderful mother, like her mother, Ava. With no particular career in mind, she sees how her mother

The Characters and the Setting

has helped her family, and intends to follow that good example. The quarrels Mia has with her older brother, Daniel, mean little. A typical older brother, Daniel has given Mia ample reason to be annoyed with him, but she knows she loves her brother, and her parents of course. Mia admires both parents. Their service to others in the ministry means a great deal to her.

THE SETTING

The Martinez family has been called from a mid-sized city to plant a church in a similar city. Their new location is a mid-sized city centered in a largely rural area. The new city has an agricultural heritage, but has developed as will be described by some of the narratives. There is some diversity in jobs and activities. The new location is some distance from their previous home. Transition is possible, and not necessarily abrupt, but eventually they will be forced to move, and find new jobs. The teenage children will enroll in a new school system. Visiting family and friends is reasonably possible, but not convenient.

The Journey Begins

Answering the Call

As it is, and as it must be, with every spiritual calling, this journey began with prayer. At its inception, and with each step of the journey, prayer has been the key, essential element. There is more, so much more. Praise of course. Faith. Struggle. Risk. Mistakes. Determination. Joy, abundant, abiding joy. Fellowship. Accomplishment. Humility. His glorious presence.

I stop, for there is a story that must be told. It is a new story, yet it is not. It is understood by so many who have answered this call to plant a church. For them, this story will resonate in their souls. There are stories for each element there is capacity to describe. The story will unfold to His glory. As has been said, it began with prayer.

A devoted follower of Jesus, and even as early as childhood, in prayer I proclaimed my willingness to obey Him and follow His leading. "No sacrifice was too great. Wherever you lead, I will follow", I said in so many calls to consecration. The simplicity of such consecration was enduring and compelling. It was more than emotion, for emotion fades. But this feeling remained. There was a point where that consecration took root. It grew as I matured. It was no longer a distant reaching for the future. It was present now, and it had substance. The root took shape. Consecration became calling. Consecration and sacrifice were no longer theoretical; they were practical, personal and pointed.

So it was for me and Ava, the church planters. By His grace, He gave us the courage and commitment to keep pursuing. And in that pursuit, our continuing prayers revealed God's determination. His will and His presence were the same. His persistence became manifest as we sought Him. It was mutual. This determined will was not an individual calling, unknown to the other. God called us both. That voice, that persistence, and that determination called us to complete what we had long professed in private and joint devotion. He called us to align with and submit to His will. When Ava and I shared what we both had known alone, we found there was no confusion and no separation. His voice was one. We had been called to plant a church.

    The burden was unmistakable. It was unshakable. The certainty of His calling was ever more persistent and determined. But it was not an unwelcome weight. Though heavy, this burden was somehow welcome. There was joy, but it was not lighthearted. It was sobering to be sure. There was an accompanied sacredness. That sacred voice brought deep, certain joy. This was what we sought. It was the will for which we had so long prayed.

    While that is true, there was still uncertainty. We had all confidence in Him. That was firmly settled. No, the uncertainty was in us. We were, at times, uncertain of the calling. Yes, it was sacred, but was it real? Was it generated by our emotion? It was sensed by both of us, and that seemed like proof enough. But was there some kind of sympathetic longing that forced us to join in an emotional yoke that wasn't His leading after all? And even if those answers affirmed that this was real, there were still questions about us. There were so many reasons to doubt. This was simply more than we were able to do. Ava and I confessed,

Answering the Call

"We aren't prepared. We aren't worthy. And we certainly aren't qualified."

But the certainty of that call, thankfully, drove us to respond. The newness of the calling had to be solidified. We needed something more concrete to cement that leading. We made a few visits to the city for which we were burdened. That exposure produced a predictable result. Our burden grew. The calling was no longer detached. We had witnessed our "field", and the call of the harvest drew us. The need was realized. It did not wane. To the contrary, it grew ever stronger. As we continued in prayer and fasting, so grew our confidence that this was, in fact, God's will. Counsel only strengthened what already seemed certain.

As the uncertainty had come before, our own analysis brought more questions. "How can we do this?" This time the question wasn't so much about us. What He wanted to accomplish seemed, at least to some extent, clear. But how to do it was an entirely different thing. In simple vernacular, we were clueless. Again, we confessed, "Lord, we don't even know what the first step is. We certainly don't have a sequence of things that would lead us to this known, predictable outcome. HELP!"

In the midst of those new questions, it was almost as if a spirit took over. In truth, that is what happened. In our confusion and devotion, His spirit transformed our thinking. We began to look at it positively. Instead of seeing what couldn't be done, we asked a new question, "What CAN be done?" Instead of questioning with bewilderment how to set a course, we began with calmness to identify the steps we

Answering the Call

could take. The Lord would lead us and correct those steps, but respond we would. That lesson was echoed so many times as we continued. Instead of a series of seemingly unending questions with no answers, after identifying what we could do, we assessed what the next questions were, wrote them down, and came up with a plan for how, who or where we could get answers. Doubt was being transformed.

We had no choice but to say yes. It wasn't a vague affirmation of accepting His will in some generic sense. It was a specific answer of "yes" to a specific calling. We would take this big step. We would answer the call.

As difficult as it was to get to that submission, saying "yes" was followed by communication and consultation with others. We began by telling our "inner circle", our family and close friends. As we would learn, we were not isolated pilgrims without support.

Our calling was not without accountability. I told Ava, "We need approval if we're going to do this. We must make an application and meet with the District Board for their approval. God has placed them in leadership, and we should respect their leadership, their guidance, and their counsel."

Part of that also meant getting feedback. There was feedback from family and friends. They proved to be the spiritual champions that we needed, for over and over we found we could count on their prayers and support. Our pastor was the spiritual strength we knew him to be. What he said in the pulpit was what he was in person. He was a man of faith, leading us in ours.

Answering the Call

Recognizing and respecting their authority, we were nervous about our application to the District Board. Feedback took on a different meaning. I questioned, "Will we be told to wait? Is there something that, in their wisdom, will thwart what we know, from our perspective, to be our calling?" Their prayerful, and somewhat deliberate, process once again forced us to accept God's will. Ava respectfully acknowledged, "Edwin, it's out of our hands."

In a few nervous weeks, we had our answer. We had been approved! As we announced that approval, our satisfaction was great. Nearly everyone to whom we spoke was supportive. Some expressed concerns, but none was obstructive. For now, all that mattered was that this step was complete. There would be so much more, as we shall see. But we rested for a while in the comfort and assurance that we would soon pursue our calling.

Answering the call was not an easy continuation of what we were already doing. It would demand a complete change in our lives. And it was more than my life and Ava's life. Our family was called to this new city. Daniel and Mia were not an incidental commodity in the calling. They were a key element of that vision. We were responsible for the direction of our family, but we could not simply ignore our children's concerns. They were warranted. They had questions, and so did we. "How will they change?" "Is this a good place to raise children?" "Will they resent God for taking them from their friends and what they know?" Will this draw them to God, or will this change start a spiral that leads them away from God?" "God, we're sure about us, but is this good for our children?"

Answering the Call

As the initial excitement faded, Ava and I also began to recognize the reality that would soon be upon us. Yes, our lives would be dramatically different. Away from the children, I expressed that realization, "Now we feel safe. We have a routine, jobs, and the kids are happy with the church and school. That is all about to change."

There was, with that growing recognition, an uneasy sense of impending isolation. We would be alone. That's what our feelings were telling us. Everything that gave us security would be replaced. We would have to find a new home, get new jobs, enroll Daniel and Mia and participate as parents in a new school. There was rhythm, a schedule that was familiar to us. Yes, we knew a new rhythm would develop, but that seemed distant. Until then, control would be lost.

Change and denial are common companions. We weren't there yet. Yes, we had announced our calling and our approval. We had garnered support of many. But --- "What if we don't go?" "Was it too late?" The reasons to stay seemed obvious. The fears resurfaced. It was a temptation of the devil. But it provoked us again. To restate all of them is to do injustice to His marvelous work.

Though real and strong for a short time, we could not dismiss the gravity of such a mistake. In His great grace, He allowed us to see beyond it. It was a vision with people and voices. It was the questions that would haunt us forever. "What are the consequences of not responding to His leading? "What about our friends and family who have given their support?" "Will anyone trust us again?" There would be unending, haunting questions about missing the will of God.

Answering the Call

"What would our lives have been like if we had said yes?" "Will there be regret for the rest of our lives?" The answer was clear. He had called us. The paralysis of fear was not an acceptable response.

Our final step in answering the call was getting started. It would not be accomplished quickly or without effort, but we started.

We began looking for a new home. That meant putting our house up for sale, and possibly storing things until we moved into the new home.

We began the transition to new job(s). In the interim, we kept our old jobs. Once moved, that would mean driving longer, but the financial security was worth that cost. That also meant that while spending more time getting to and from work, we would have to find time to look for new jobs.

As soon as we were moved, we would enroll the children in their new school. Waiting until then seemed irresponsible of us and thoughtless regarding the children, so we talked to the school to find out how to make that transition. By so doing, they helped us to get a head start, and even provided opportunity for Daniel and Mia to get acquainted with their "new friends".

There were many other things. Some were expected; many were not. But we now could say, "We answered the call."

Answering the Call

READING GUIDE POINTS:
1. Spiritual calling begins with prayer
2. As consecration develops, it becomes personal and specific
3. Calling is accompanied by accountability
4. God calls all of your family
5. Initially, calling is accompanied with uncertainty and isolation
6. Saying "yes" requires action
7. Responding is often a determined and nervous process of transition

References from:
Effective Christianity: Managing Life's Projects

- Chapter 3, page 25
  - Each calling is personal
    - It is unique
    - Comparing to others is unwise
- Chapter 4, page 31
  - Nothing can replace anointing. It is undeniable and self-confirming.
- Chapter 4, page 32
  - Hunger for His will causes you to long for the dream He's put in your heart
- Chapter 4, page 36
  - Spiritual fulfillment requires responding, and taking action when God leads you
- Chapter 4, page 37
  - Fulfilment requires risk
    - People who avoid risk end up accomplishing very little or nothing
    - Avoiding mistakes is impossible if you are going to succeed
    - Fulfillment is more important than risk, mistakes and embarrassment

A Sure Foundation

When I was a boy, we would visit my aunt and uncle. To be clear, the uncle was my mom's brother. I had other uncles, but this memory goes with him.

I was always excited to visit them. They were so happy to see us. Mom loved being with her brother. To us, it was just natural to enjoy being with your family. Mom and my uncle would share stories of their childhood. Listening to them now, it seemed magical. Time must change how you remember things. Though they laughed with fondness, some of the stories made me wonder how they could still love each other. It was hard to believe that these two loving adults once acted much differently. Most of the stories weren't like that, but some of their tales were interesting. Somehow it was a pleasant bond they shared. It had nothing to do with dad, but he seemed to understand. They both would say, "Just wait. Edwin, one day, you and your sister will look back and laugh too. You don't see it, but we see now much you love each other." I doubted it then; I know it now.

My aunt and uncle's farm had woods nearby. All of it provided a great place to play with my cousins. At this stage in my life, it meant playing with someone other than my sister.

There was a special place in those woods. For in it was our favorite creek. It was away from the noises of homes and crowds. It had sandy banks and rock walls. There were trees that had somehow rooted themselves in rock that seemed impenetrable. There were pleasant sounds of birds, and other

A Sure Foundation

noises that gave us pause, but not for long. It was a cool and refreshing place. And we could be whatever we wanted to be.

In the spring time, heavy rains would sometimes bring high, cold water to that creek. In the hot summer, the coolness or the creek would be refreshing. But falling into the water in the spring would be the end of what should have been a great day. In the spring, the water was too cold. Great adventure loomed, but it wasn't in the water. This high water was a barrier to overcome.

Someone would say, "We need a bridge to get by. There are boards and branches already across the creek." This was proof that others had taken this path before. There were many stones, but too many were slippery and unstable. The branches were broken and could roll with the slightest step. It seemed that boards, being flat, would be perfect. Often, though, they were placed on rounded rocks, and they too would turn easily.

We needed steps that were stable. We were looking for things of which we were certain.

Not all had planted a sure foundation to reach the other side. Were these branches, these boards, and these stones secure? Maybe so, but often many were not. It was a certain destination, but now an uncertain path. We needed things that we could count on through our spring peril.

There was risk of falling in, risk of falling, and risk of getting hurt. Cuts and bruises were certain results, and broken bones were possible.

A Sure Foundation

Surety and laxity don't exist well together. To be sure would have required effort and delay. The easy, lazy response said, "Don't worry about it. Go ahead. It's not the worth the trouble. Is it really necessary to fix it? How much work will it take? How long will we be delayed?" Or should we have taken the risk? After all, we hadn't come to fix a bridge. We had other, more important things in mind.

If we made the path sure, we would fulfill the dream we envisioned. If not, we risked failure.

We could have turned back I suppose. But suppose it would have to be, for I can't remember a time when we did turn back. We were determined. It was worth the risk to cross. If we fell in, we would deal with the consequences. But then we realized, it was worth the effort to make sure.

I was reminded how it felt as a boy at my aunt and uncle's farm, in the woods, and by the creek. It felt like spring time when the waters were high. We needed things that were certain.

When Ava and I first answered the call to plant a church, we honestly weren't certain about anything other than the call itself. Since that first moment, the Lord began to impress on us the importance of three fundamentals. At the outset, they were the things that were certain. Two we knew; one had to be developed. First, we had faith in the Name of the Lord. Second, we had faith in His Word. Third, we determined to build strong, foundational families. These were those components of the sure foundation.

A Sure Foundation

With that being the foundation, we set ourselves on a simple strategy. It wasn't just a strategy for me and Ava. Early, we rehearsed this strategy to Daniel and Mia. We repeated it often. "Proclaim the Name, proclaim the Word, and establish key, foundational families."

Planting a church wasn't just about having a church building and a name. Actually, it wasn't about attendance and offerings either. All of those were necessary, but at the core, we were furthering faith. We were called to a great spiritual responsibility, and faith had to be the core. It is the Gospel, the Word and the Name that are effective. We did not trust in our own abilities. We had already proven to ourselves that we were unqualified. But faith displaced this inward focus. We trusted in Him. The Church and this church would be established in the Name of Jesus and in the Word of God.

Ava and I took turns saying the same thing, "We are called as missionaries. As strongly as missionaries that are called to nations in other lands and of other languages, we are called to this city. As missionaries, we know that call is to be a voice for the Name and a voice for the Word."

We knew there would be challenges. We believed that key families would sustain the church through those challenges. We would count on that steadfastness.

Our target was to establish strong relationships with at least three families. These few, important resources would be the foundation of the church. We were planting a church; plants need strong roots. These families were those roots.

A Sure Foundation

We had many reasons to appreciate their role. They were roots, they were disciples, and they brought strength. As roots, they would help us endure. They would become the keys to discipleship as well. Before there was a launch team or focused evangelism, they were disciples. They were establishing the foundation for launch and discipleship. They were a source of strength to our family. I remember saying to Ava, "I'm so thankful for these foundational pillars. Their support and faithfulness give me strength when I struggle. I know they strengthen you too. But it's more than that. Our children need other mature, adult role models. They need other children that are be faithful peers. These foundational families provide that." As we were tested, Ava and I, our children and these foundational families were to remain sure and united.

Thank the Lord, He gave us a sure foundation. His Name is sure. His Word is sure. These foundational families were sure as well.

READING GUIDE POINTS:
1. The most important element of a sure foundation is to be absolutely certain of your calling
2. The biggest risk is not the calling, but the path you choose to fulfill it
3. A sure foundation is built on faith in the Name of the Lord
4. A sure foundation is built on faith in His Word
5. A sure foundation is built on a determination to build strong, foundational families

A Sure Foundation

> **References from:**
> ***Effective Christianity: Managing Life's Projects***
> - Chapter 1, page 2
>   - Keep first things first
>   - Nothing else replaces the responsibility of sound doctrine, right values and the Word
> - Chapter 1, page 9
>   - Everything must be bult on a strong foundation
> - Chapter 2, page 11
>   - Spiritual priorities cannot be compromised

Matters of the Heart

Beware of the Lone Wolf

Wow! Suddenly, we were there. We had moved to the city of our calling. The anxiety and uncertainty of answering the call and the determination not to retreat from that calling took courage and faith, but until now, it had all been about the future. The questions were about what WOULD happen. It was the FUTURE that was uncertain. But all of that changed. We were there. It wasn't about the future any more. Yes, there was a future. But it was no longer about where we were going to be. It had become an extension of where we now were.

Some things were still without question. We were sure of the message. That faith was sure. As we had professed with confidence, we still firmly stood. We would proclaim His Name, and His Word. Our calling was not in question. Those doubts and anxieties were behind. We were there, committed to moving forward. Recognizing this, I said, "Moving forward is no longer just a plan. It's time to act." We had listed actions we would take. We could have moved strongly, and maybe blindly, ahead with those predetermined actions. But this was our last chance to make sure. "Were those really the right first steps?", I asked. We couldn't have known then what early steps might be irreversible. But doing nothing was not an option.

Those first few days we felt so all alone. We were a family. We had each other, but who else was there? We were drawn to each other, but even in that bond, individually, we each felt isolated.

I wanted to feel like a lion. Female and young lions are part of a collective called a pride. But adult males, especially

Beware of the Lone Wolf

the strong ones, are solitary symbols of strength. They dominate in solitude.

I felt more like a lone wolf. Usually, wolves join together. Those who spend time in the wilderness know that a wolf pack is one of the most effective and dangerous things you could face. You don't want to compete with a pack of wolves. Few who do survive.

A lone wolf, though, is a solitary creature. For a number of reasons, some wolves leave the security of the pack. They must fight alone for their own survival. The wilderness may no longer be to their advantage; as with those that had been their prey, the wilderness becomes a threat to them as well. A lone wolf loses the protection of the community. Lone wolves have to figure everything out by themselves. There is no team strategy for conquest. There is no security from the group. In its isolation, a lone wolf is more likely to die.

Clearly, we needed connections, and we needed them soon. The truth was that we already had established some connections, and realized quickly that they were needed. We had identified potential mentors early that we knew wanted to help. Thankfully, we had listened to these mentors, and started building other networks before we moved.

The first was a network of friends, family and peers. We had even established a means of communicating what and how we were doing. We were so thankful. These people saved us. We wanted to be strong. We didn't want to rely on them so quickly, but those feelings of isolation dashed any pride that held us back. Having that connection was more important than we realized.

Beware of the Lone Wolf

The second was a network of prayer. Ava lamented, "This isn't supposed to be about us. There will be plenty of 'spiritual' needs to present to our prayer network later. I know that's the goal. It's supposed to be about the mission and achieving results through the power of prayer." But again, pride was dashed. The first request was made: pray for us.

Few of our connections were collective. Most of them were personal. In this regard, we weren't just a team that needed weekly group meetings; we were individuals that each needed personal connections.

As soon as possible, I began talking to those that had done this before. Their experience was relevant. They could listen, and I knew they understood. Some said, "I know exactly where you are. I've already been there." Their counsel was immeasurable.

Ava needed ongoing fellowship. She had regular meetings with friends and mentors. On occasion, she would visit them as well. It was important to get away, even briefly. The personal contact revived her.

Daniel and Mia needed connections too. They made contact regularly with some of their old friends. Though we had moved, we tried not to cut them off completely from their past, and the security it brought. In fact, we encouraged them to visit their friends. This transition made us more mobile. We hadn't planned on being separated from our children, but their well-being sometimes necessitated it.

Then there was the familiarity of activities we had enjoyed before. Mia asked, "Dad, will we ever get to go anywhere again?" With fatherly assurance, I replied, "We may live somewhere else, but we are still a family. We will go to conferences, seminars and camps. Life hasn't stopped just because we've been called to plant a church."

All of that was about staying connected to the past. But we also needed to connect with our future. We need to connect with new people. This forced some behavior that seemed unnatural at times. We were all forced to break out of our shells and talk to people more than had been our custom in the past. The connections themselves weren't as natural either. We had to start looking for opportunities to connect with new people.

Connections were no longer haphazard; they were intentional. Meetings were not accidental; there was design for them. It was now part of our calling. God was orchestrating His purpose. He was leading them to us, and leading us to them. He was preparing their hearts to meet us. Out meeting wasn't just His will for us; it was also His will for them.

We prayed about our connections, "Lord, guide us to meet the right people." We continued to pray for them after we met, "Jesus, give us a Spirit-led boldness. Give us divine confidence." It wasn't a confidence in us that we sought, but a confidence in the Lord and His calling. In nearly every prayer, I acknowledged my need of Him, "I'm not qualified. I don't have all of the skills. It isn't about me. It's about you. You can equip us. You will qualify us."

We did our best to follow-up with everyone we could. Connecting with these people was why we were there. That meant, as much as possible, following through on everything we said we would do. We kept notes so we wouldn't forget.

If we were to maximize connections, we tried to do as much of our business as we could in our new city. Yes, we had familiar stores from before, but those people weren't here. We even got involved with the Chamber of Commerce. They were always looking for people to be ambassadors at events in the community. What better opportunity to connect. This "business" connection helped us to become known as people who were involved and cared about the community.

All of this community connection needed to be honest. We had to respect that there were other important things in the community. We needed to appreciate people who were involved and cared for others. It would have been selfish to only be concerned only about what happened at our church.

One of the easiest things to do was connect at restaurants. We were no longer there just to eat and demand good service. We were looking for opportunity to connect with someone.

I had heard stories about this before, but couldn't image it happening to us. We were being served in a restaurant, but the server wasn't really paying attention. We had to repeat ourselves when ordering. And as should have been expected, not everything was right when it was delivered.

I had to give credit to Ava. She sensed something, "I think something is wrong with that poor girl." It was the Lord directing her, of course. We were reminded of those prayers for our connections. Rather than scold her, Ava asked her, "Is everything all right?" A tear appeared in her eye immediately, "I just got the news that my dad has been in an accident, and probably wouldn't make it through the night. As soon as I can, I'm heading to the hospital."

With compassion, I said, "My wife and I are in the ministry. May we pray for you? Would you like for us to go with you to the hospital." Without hesitation, she said yes to both questions. She did see her father, but sadly, he passed from his injuries.

But we continued to pray with her. In a few weeks, we started a home Bible study with her family. We had faith in God's Word from the outset. We believed it would bear fruit. Soon after the home Bible study, she and her family came to church. In a short while, she and her husband were baptized in the name of Jesus, and they received the Holy Ghost. They were faithful members, and we were all thankful.

As important as worship services, Bible studies and finding a location for the church were, we realized that we first had to focus on connections. What these new believers would need was connection. They needed to connect with us and other foundational families in the church. Doctrine was important, and it would come. I had to admit to Ava, "Until we are established, coffee may be more important to them than a deep Bible study." It was hard to admit, but at that early stage, relationships were more important than preaching. We had to focus on friendship, relationship, and connection.

What we found was that we didn't have to go on our own. We didn't need to be lone wolves. Others were ready to help. And help they did. They helped with support. Important feedback from our family, our old networks and our new contacts helped as well.

We might have wished that we had seen things differently, and been spared that period of loneliness. But it taught us lessons. We were able to identify with people in their loneliness. That too was an important connection, for every person has periods where they feel alone.

Beware of the Lone Wolf

As we pursued connections with determination, word spread about us and our church. No church is without opposition. Whether it came from the church or from the community, when opposition came, there were people to support us.

With encouragement in her voice, Ava reinforced what we always knew but didn't always feel, "Edwin, we were never alone after all. The Lord was always with us." It sounds like a cliché, but even cliches are true. Of course, the strength from the Lord was essential, but it was more than the Lord. We had a network of people who brought comfort and solace in struggle. There were many people whose faithfulness helped sustain us. It came from people we knew, and people we were yet to know. The community was bigger than we realized. It only grew bigger and stronger.

READING GUIDE POINTS:
1. A feeling of isolation is common when transitioning to your new location
2. Solitude is dangerous
3. Maintain connections with friends, family and peers
4. Build a network of prayer partners
5. Carefully balance connections to your past with connections to your future
6. Be intentional, determined and prayerful in creating new connections
7. New converts also need connections
8. People will help you. You are not alone.

Beware of the Lone Wolf

> **References from:**
> ***Effective Christianity: Managing Life's Projects***
> - Chapter 2, page 13
>   - Practical steps are required to be spiritually effective
> - Chapter 2, page 14
>   - Growth forces us to change how we think
> - Chapter 5, pages 48-51
>   - Share with your connections
>   - Vision
>   - Plan
>   - Risks
>   - Improvements/help needed
>   - Don't take this all on yourself, all alone
>   - Trust others
>   - Be honest
>   - Welcome feedback and help

The Evolution of Vision

As a young man, I took trips into a wilderness area nearby. It was undeveloped land. There were no cities. Homes were far apart. Neighbors were distant. Those who lived there must have enjoyed isolated tranquility. Those self-reliant found refuge. Few conveniences existed. But convenience was not the goal. It was rustic. It wasn't suitable for most travelers, unless you enjoyed primitive camping.

I have talked about visiting my aunt and uncle's farm already. But that was different. Those were boyhood memories. I was now a young man. That was family. This was not.

I remember the first trip. It was just after I graduated from high school. In many ways, it was a big chance for me. I could establish my independence. I would prove that I could take care of myself.

This was a big chance in other ways as well. I had never been there before. There was excitement. It would be an adventure. I had envisioned what it would be like, but I hadn't yet seen it.

My directions led me away from those things most familiar – my family and home. Very quickly, the town where we lived was now behind me. But that was not my concern. My destination was in the distance, on the horizon. It seemed so far away. Nothing was distinct yet. There had been many dreams of what I would see and what I would do when I got there. But for now, I was neither in the past that could be seen in my mirror. Nor was I in the future I had foreseen. I was in the moment. The only goal, at this stage, was to get there.

The Evolution of Vision

As I got closer, the destination began to take shape. It was becoming clearer. Things I could not see before, I was now beginning to see. The goal was changing. Just getting there was no longer enough.

Drawing closer still, I began to see caves, cracks in the rocks and the color of the stones. Trees started to appear. There were large trees in the meadows. They were straight and tall. On the hills, the trees were different. They were small and twisted, conforming to more harsh surroundings. There were streams and flowers, steep cliffs and embankments. A few clouds dotted the sky. Hawks would soar in the sky. Continuing closer, mountain animals, like goats, could be seen on the peaks. Then in the meadow, if I was lucky, I would see deer. Would there be rabbits or foxes? What else would be seen? This only added wonder to the excitement.

My car would only get me so far. Then I would have to finish on foot. The trail was windy and uneven. There was gear for sleeping and supplies to bear. It became evident that getting to the final destination would not be easy. This laborious end was not part of the fascination I had envisioned. After the long journey, the last steps would still be challenging. But it was necessary if I would see the fulfillment of my dream.

With great exertion and an accompanying endurance, I completed the final leg of the journey. Though exhausted, I was excited and enthralled with the knowledge that I was nearly there. Soon my imagination would become reality.

My arrival at the chosen site was a confirmation. A milestone had been achieved. At least for a few moments, it was time to rest and enjoy the accomplishment of a goal long

The Evolution of Vision

sought, that was achieved with great ardor. There had been a few surprises and it took more work than I had planned, but I was satisfied.

Getting there, though, was only a new beginning. How would I sustain myself for the next few days? Where would I get those things necessary to survive? Surely these questions were unnecessary. I had given it thought beforehand, and had done my best to plan responsibly. The fruit of my planning was about to be proven.

Thinking back, it shouldn't have been a surprise that I learned much from that first trip. To expect anything else wasn't realistic. Yes, as I was able, I had done what I could. But I had never done this, nor had I had ever been here before. Of course, then, those first, few days were filled with some struggle as I realized there were things I had overlooked. But it was only the first trip. The next trips would be better. I would be smarter. I would learn from those mistakes.

The first lesson was this. You must learn to adapt to survive in the wilderness. That was probably the most important lesson learned. Things wouldn't all go as planned. I made mistakes. Reality forced me to adapt. Adapt or fail is an unbending reality. Fortunately, I was able to adapt. I did survive. More than that, I could now tell the story with great fondness.

Fortunately, there was a backup plan. It sems obvious now, but risk and responsibility required that there be alternatives. Remember that I was establishing my independence. Certainly, there was some truth to that. The onset was a solitary, exciting trip. But it would not be so for long. Others would come later. I was abler to communicate and survive until they could bring what I had missed. What I lacked, they provided. Being the first to arrive was rewarding. Not being alone was essential for survival.

Soon thereafter, I could say that I was a lot smarter. My experience had taught me what things I would need. I knew where I could go, and where I should not. Being without was a great teacher. After that first trip, there were some things that I would never forget again. I also learned that there are things that should only be attempted with friends. Being alone in the wilderness had a sense of majesty. But it was only short-lived. Companionship brought assurance, and a shared journey was a strong bond that no one else could quite appreciate.

This journey of planting a church has been much like that first trip. At first, there was mostly excitement, emotion, and imagination. Ava and I didn't and couldn't really know how it would unfold, or what we would encounter. Our initial perspective was expectant, while at the same time, unfocused and, for a while, undefined. The approach, though, was both positive and pure.

As it was with the trip to the desert, clarity would come as we got nearer. The vision would evolve. What was initially only imagined became a vision with substance. Clarity changes inversely with distance; it grows as the destination nears.

At this early stage, we were still at some midpoint in the process. Many things had already become clearer. Many more, though, were not only unclear; they were still unknown. We couldn't yet see the streams, flowers and animals. Those things would appear later. But what we could see was exciting and beautiful.

The Evolution of Vision

The confirmation we had found thus far fulfilled our call to the journey. At the same time, it was the catalyst for what now seemed to be a new journey. We were compelled to continue. It was still new. There was still a future marked with uncertainty. Still, it was as raw, exciting, and as pure as its predecessor.

We engaged ourselves in the continuing, yet new challenge. This was that first trip. Lessons would be learned. Mistakes would be many, and corrections would seem unending. The learning was unique. For so much of what we learned could only have been taught by this experience. But sustaining the vision required the same things as before. We had to adapt. We had to change.

We were engaged in a transformation. Our vision was steadily evolving. As it was with all of our activity, vision itself was transformed from being raw, undefined and unfocused. Clarity was emerging. Each time we achieved some milestone, vision was renewed afresh. This transformation of vision didn't confuse or frustrate us. To the contrary, our role, our passion, and His presence became only stronger. Through this mystery of learning, I would tell Ava, "My commitment to this divine end has not waned. As the vision becomes clearer, I became more and more determined." God was revealing a new, deeper understanding of His will. Fulfilling His purpose was not an option. And only we could know what that fulfillment would mean.

Each step was part of an evolution of maturity. Vision was our bounty for listening, and putting ourselves in a place to grow. We grew beyond what we could ever have imagined. Maturity was the inevitable, and unplanned catalyst. Maturity itself was not our goal in our seeking. But what we sought

The Evolution of Vision

was unachievable without it. Our vision evolved in accordance with our maturity.

None of that was possible without His presence. We were not alone. With a sense of thanksgiving, Ava would say, "Edwin, through each step, we have seen that His hand has guided us."

It brought, though, an intriguing question. We were not done. There was still much to do to plant a church. Our vision had evolved and grown as we matured. Seeing what had happened so far had bought intriguing fascination, which caused me to wonder, "Where will this vision take us now?

READING GUIDE POINTS:
1. Getting started is the first step toward the vision
2. There will be many surprises and things you must learn
3. It is the journey that makes the vision more clear
4. You must adapt to survive
5. The confirmation the journey brings compels you to continue
6. The evolution of vision is coupled with the inevitable, unplanned maturity forced upon you
7. The transformation of vision makes your commitment stronger
8. Recognize His presence and guidance

The Evolution of Vision

> **References from:**
> ***Effective Christianity: Managing Life's Projects***
> - Chapter 7, page 71
>   - Recognize your vision
> - Chapter 7, page 72
>   - Know your vision
>   - Obey your vision
> - Chapter 7, page 73
>   - Be transparent
> - Chapter 7, pages 73-74
>   - Hold nothing back
> - Chapter 7, page 74
>   - Share in the success
>   - Keep the right focus
>   - Stick to the right values
> - Chapter 7, page 75
>   - Persevere in the vision as it evolves

Connecting (Your Community)

Introductory remarks from the lady in this relationship:

Edwin and I complement each other well. Even when we agree with each other, we see things differently. Edwin often says that to get another perspective, he doesn't have to leave the house. We've taken personality tests to see what it says about us. Invariably, we are on opposite sides of the scale. It doesn't trouble us. We find it's a strength. We respect our differences, and usually find the right balance.

To be clear, this is not Edwin's calling; it is ours. The Lord dealt with my heart, and confirmed that He was calling me, and not just him. We are a team, determined as partners to follow what burns in my heart.

We have worked on many things together. The long-term plan was a joint effort. My husband is committed, and driven to see things happen. Sometimes, I was the voice of realism. I can be blinded by my emotions and feelings. Even compassion must be controlled. He can be blinded by his passionate determination. Here we tried to have balance. Especially for the portion of the long-term plan that dealt with our family, we worked together. My voice meant something. My heart stirred for my children as they expressed their feelings. There were sacrifices and compromise. When it was over, I was satisfied. In my soul, I knew it was right. We had talked. I wanted to hear my husband. He heard me. Our children were heard. We prayed together. Most importantly, we listened to the Lord. He was there. The Lord has guided us. I have trusted Him to lead us.

As a pastor's wife, I have seen things from a different perspective. As a lady I will tell the story differently.

Connecting (Your Community)

One of the more difficult things was losing valued connections that meant so much to me. As much as we could, we tried to keep those bonds. Edwin and I found that we would rely on them a great deal. Our location would change, but our family would not. That bond was firm. It was secured by a strong love. The connection was part of our identity.

We stayed connected to our friends. It wasn't constant. We were busy. They were busy. But when we connected, it was as if nothing had changed. They were still our friends, and we cherished that friendship.

Surprisingly, one of the hardest separations was from my old job. I enjoyed it, but, more importantly, I enjoyed those with whom I worked. They were all my friends. We didn't go on vacations together. We didn't get together at each other's houses. But at work we were connected. We would talk about our families, trips we had planned, and our involvement in our own churches. We talked of the price of groceries and soaring utilities, and what the most recent storm had done. Money was important, but the connection with my friends meant more to me than the money.

I remember the last day on my old job. There were tears as I said goodbye to many friends. Unlike our closer, family friends, I realized I might not see these people again. Many said, "Don't be a stranger. Stay in touch." But that was going to be difficult. If I had simply changed jobs in the same city, I might see them in a store or business. But that wasn't the case. We were moving. The opportunities to reconnect would be rare. That made this moment more difficult. Someone had told us, "This transition means that a door behind you is closing." As the door closed behind me on that last day of work, I understood what that meant.

Connecting (Your Community)

Happily, though, there were many new connections to be made. There would be new friends. Places now new to us would become routine. But that would take time, and that time of distant and broken connections was hard. We were moving from "them" to "us".

Missionaries placed in a new country understood this, but being called to another city meant connecting with another culture. We may have spoken the same language, but so many things ended there. Each city has an identity. We needed to understand how these people thought. What was their history? What mattered to them? What made them proud? We couldn't think of ourselves as being in their community; this was now our community. We also needed to be proud to be part of it.

Making really strong connections would have consequences. With that commitment there was risk. We needed to make commitments so strong that it would be hard to leave. This wasn't about it being hard to leave our old place; it needed to be hard to leave our new place.

Creating effective bonds would take trust. There could be no holding back. It was about relationships. Connection required personal understanding, or it would not be effective.

Whatever my dream had been before was to be replaced by a new dream. What was before was based on connections. What was ahead would also be based on connections. We would develop life-long friendships. I told Edwin, "Some of these new friends will become as important to us as our old friends have been."

Family is so important. But those dreams too would change. I didn't yet know who these people were. That was the connecting that was yet to occur. But this would change

Connecting (Your Community)

the course of our family deeply. Daniel and Mia would probably marry within this community. If so, it would probably be with people who were not yet saved. I surprised Edwin one day with a thought that had dawned on me, "Our grandchildren will probably be born in this community." "Oh", he said. "I hadn't thought of that. You're probably right." Like missionaries in far off lands, our grandchildren would identify with this community as their home.

I was reminded of the Biblical story of Ruth. I could see myself as this great woman of the Bible. I could identify with her. Her story was about family and connections.

Ruth was called to a new people. That calling came through one person, Naomi. She could not have known at first, but Naomi would become the matriarch of her new family. Oddly, though the calling was founded in her relationship with Naomi, it was not Naomi who called her. To the contrary, Naomi urged her not to come. All those around her, and even those she was called to, told Ruth not to come. But something greater was calling her to them. And that connection would make an irreversible and eternal impact on her as a mother and the family that would become her heritage. She would leave her homeland, and identify completely with a new people. They became her family. Her children were part of this new people. Her children's heritage was now joined to theirs. She never turned back. There was an anointing that sent her, and an anointing through the connections she was led to establish. Those connections were directed by God. I shared my revelation with my husband, "It's not just about Ruth. Who her children would meet, who they would love, and who they would marry were the result of this God-ordained separation from her past, and this God-

Connecting (Your Community)

ordained connection with her future. Both the separation and the connection were ordained. Her heritage as a mother was sealed with eternal impact. Through her, because she accepted her call, separated herself from a past that was familiar, and connected with her new people, a Messiah would come. Jesus was born through her."

Ruth identified completely with her new community. Edwin and I created a plan to make connections with ours. My husband valued the plan; I valued connection. Together, it worked. Once again, we were a great team. We had to decide where we would go, and what we would say.

We listed businesses for connection. Where we would do business? Where would we be customers? What other businesses could we target? Connecting with the Chamber of Commerce was part of the plan.

Then we had to decide where we would eat. While eating at a restaurant one day, I said to the family, "This kind of structure, deciding where we will eat, seemed over the top at first. But I guess it does make sense. We have to be intentional." Edwin replied, "We won't just go to our favorite restaurants. We will intentionally spread ourselves to make as many connections and friends as we can." That also meant doing more than eating; we intended to have conversation with employees and customers. As you can imagine, Mia had no problem with the conversation part. Daniel, on the other hand, took more coaxing.

However, Daniel had taken a business class. In it, he learned about the "elevator speech". When he first mentioned it, I laughed. I wasn't supposed to laugh at my son. It sounded so funny. But when Damiel explained it, I realized that he was pretty smart after all, and that he was

Connecting (Your Community)

willing to do his part in reaching this city. He said, "An elevator speech is a message you practice to get your point across in the amount of time you would have with someone in an elevator. It can be about a business, a product, a project, or just an idea or argument." With that new found awareness, we developed our own "elevator speech".

Not every connection was personal. Some methods would leave information and hope it would take root. We created a business card, a tract, and some flyers, putting them in places that were allowed and would see good traffic.

Then it started to become more like the long-term plan we had developed. Again, balance was important. It took some time to figure it out. We had to answer some questions. We started to state them out loud. They came so fast, we had to slow down so we could write them down. "Why are we doing all of this? How do we want the community to know us? What do we want their image of us to be as a member of this community? Looking forward, where should we be in this connection plan when we announce our launch plan? What will it take to be there on time?"

It forced us to take another look at the long-term plan. We knew we would have to be flexible at times. Would this be one of those times? I asked Edwin, "Does that long-term plan have some kind of strategic objective for how our church will be connected to the community?" His answer was, "I guess it's somewhere between 'yes' and 'maybe'." The long-term plan had talked about things that would connect in the community, but it wasn't really talking about connecting. We realized it could be better.

Plans and goals were important. For me, though, it still came back to some simple things. The church and salvation

Connecting (Your Community)

itself are about connections. We had to do our part to connect and draw people to the church. That was the starting point. But it was only that. I truly valued personal connection, but this had to be more, "If they only connect with us, we will fail. We're leading them to Jesus. He's the one they need. Being connected to Jesus is what matters most." Once again, Edwin's words gave me great encouragement, "I can't say it any better than that."

This simple, basic understanding wasn't a little thing. It was important, and tied to everything else. We couldn't do all of this by ourselves. My husband had talked about the lone wolf. I said to him, "Edwin, we both know that a lone wolf mentality won't work. Connecting is part of our vision and passion. It's tied to all of the things we've been talking about: His mercy, our responsibility, the call of hungry people, and understanding what they needed. It all fits together." We were certain that great and enduring things would be established because of the connections we would make with these new people. It would ultimately be the starting point for reproduction.

Connecting (Your Community)

READING GUIDE POINTS:
1. Commitment to your calling will require you to separate from the stability and convenience of your past
2. You must identify completely with your new culture. "Them" becomes "us".
3. Your separations and new connections are both ordained
4. The new bonds you create will change you and your family
5. Your dreams will also change
6. Your church's long-term plan should clearly state how our church will be connected to the community
7. Plan how and with whom you will connect
8. The ultimate goal is to connect people with Jesus
9. Connecting is part of your vision and passion

References from:
Effective Christianity: Managing Life's Projects
- Chapter 5, page 49
  - You must share your vision for others to understand and follow
  - When the plan is clear, others can support it
- Chapter 5, page 51
  - We need others, their ideas and support. They need to know we will listen, and welcome their input. If we do, we will grow, and be more effective.

Being Consumed with Passion

The older I get, the better I understand my dad.

It was easier to understand mom. Her emotions were clear. They were strong. The depth of her devotion and the strength of her passion were undisguised.

Dad, on the other hand, was harder to read. He was strong. I knew he loved me, but he didn't show it as simply as mom. When dad said "no", it was different. We could reason with mom. She seemed to listen. Mom would often explain the reason why. Dad, on the other hand, was more resolute. Most of the time, he felt no need to explain.

It seemed that whenever mom said "yes" or "no", it was based on her care for us. We never questioned whether mom cared.

When dad said no, there always was some principle that was more important than anything else. Sometimes I felt that he didn't care. It seemed all he cared about were these "principles". "What about us?" "Aren't we important?" "Isn't there a principle about that?"

There's an example that made this point real. Actually, it's two related examples that seem to go together.

When I was reasonably young, maybe ten years old, I heard of a game that sounded fun. Some of my friends were playing it. They said it was kind of scary, like telling ghost stories. As a young boy, I had some interest in ghost stories, especially if my friends did also. It had this pointer that made the game a little bit spooky.

I went to mom, "My friends are playing this game that sounds interesting. It's kind of scary, like telling ghost stories. They say you ask questions, and then there is some kind of

Being Consumed with Passion

pointer that will point to letters and answer the question. I guess that's the spooky part. It sounds like fun. I'd like to try it. It's a weird name. They call it a Ouija Board. Can I get one?" She immediately gasped, and said, "absolutely not". I asked why. She said, "Edwin, there is evil associated with the game. It isn't just a game. There is an evil spirit attached to it. That spirit is satanic. She said that fortunately most people like it for a while, and move away. But some people get hooked on it, and it is actually spiritually dangerous." Further, she said, "The game is not new. It's been around for a long time. Your friends are too young to understand, but adults have learned, some through spiritual struggle, that it's dangerous." Then she said, "Son, the spirit that it will bring, we cannot allow in this house."

I argued a bit. "Mom, it's just a board with letters on it. How can a board be dangerous?" Somewhat patiently, she offered, "Edwin, please trust me. It's more than that. There is a spirit attached to it. It's of the devil. Trust your mother. We have to guard against allowing that kind of spirit to take hold of us."

Though I wasn't fully convinced, she did scare me, talking about evil, and the spirit of the devil. It was more than a ghost story. Maybe I could change her mind later. But for now, I would just have to tell my friends that I couldn't play. With her explanation, though, there was reason to think about it. Of course, now I thank mom for her warning. I found out later that everything she said was true.

When I was a few years older, it was probably age fourteen, there was a similar episode. Video games were becoming popular. Some friends of mine were playing one that had a lot of action. Some people were even able to play

Being Consumed with Passion

each other online. There was a shooter that would fight his way through many levels, destroying enemies, some of them demons. I didn't know a lot then, but it was becoming quite popular, and I wanted to play too. The name seemed intriguing; Doom was the name.

I mentioned it to mom, "Some of my friends are playing a computer game that has a lot of action. Some people can play each other online. You go through many levels, destroying your enemies. It's pretty popular. It's got a cool name: Doom." Her response was pretty simple, "Hmm. I don't know. You better ask your father." That was not the answer I was seeking. After a few days, though, I rehearsed the same story to dad, and asked if I could have it. He said, "Edwin, I'm not sure, but it just doesn't sound right. I heard there is this new thing called a rating system for video games. Do you know what the rating is?" "Well, no' I don't.", was my response. I really didn't know. It didn't really matter to me. My friends were playing it and I wanted to play also. "Then find out", he said.

I found it on a shelf. It said "M". I didn't really know what that meant, but it said "mature". Some of the reasons were violence and language. My heart sank a bit, but undaunted, I would try. When dad heard, he flatly said "no".

Forgetting my episode with mom about Ouija, and knowing better, I began to argue with my father. "Dad, it's just a game. It wouldn't be popular if it was evil. Games are for fun. There's nothing wrong with a game. Besides, all of my friends are playing it. Their parents allow it. So why can't I?"

I said I knew better. Dad was not sympathetic, and he didn't feel the least bit conciliatory. Mom might take time to explain, even with some patience. This was not mom!

Being Consumed with Passion

With a strong, heated response, he ended the debate. "Edwin, I said no. This is not the kind of game we will have in this house. I don't care what your friends and their parents do. They don't have the Holy Ghost. We do. I don't have to explain myself. The answer is no, and we aren't going to argue about it."

I opened my mouth. Before I could speak, dad looked right through me. At that same moment, my mother squeezed my arm in a way that spoke a warning loudly. I wasn't happy. I deserved more explanation. I wanted to do this so badly. I wasn't giving up. Yet the conversation was over. The sting was strong.

As it was with that earlier conversation with mom, the result again was no. But the conversation was much different. Mom tried to explain. With dad, there was little conversation. He rarely explained. I later realized that the game was filled with profanity, words that we would never allow otherwise in our home. The violence, to some, was captivating.

But I could only give him partial credit. Whether right or wrong, I deserved better explanation. I vowed I would never do that to my children. I wasn't going to be like him!

Years later, as a father, I started to get it. I remembered vowing I would never be like him. That thing about principles had come full circle. Of course, dad saw it. He recognized it. Sometimes, more than necessary, he would remind me of my words. Most of the time, he only smiled. For me, that was enough. That smile was an unspoken bond we shared.

I wanted to spend more time with dad while I could. I appreciated him. How much longer he would live I could not know. That time had become precious. He hadn't changed; he had only aged. My view had changed though. I no longer saw

Being Consumed with Passion

him as stubborn, frustrating and uncaring. He had become an example to me. I wanted to care for and be an example to my children as he had.

It had been said, "there's nothing like a mother's love". I wondered how many men hated the suggestion in that statement that their love was inferior.

Oh, how I loved my children. I wouldn't have ever questioned or diminished Ava's love for our children. She would say that I didn't really understand how she felt. No doubt, that was true. But equally well, I don't think she understood how I felt either. Yet, in some sense, I think she did. It may have been enough for both of us to have realized that it was more than could be expressed.

I was sure the world didn't understand how fathers loved. They surely didn't understand our heavenly Father's love. If they did, they would have embraced it without hesitation.

Mothers and fathers incessantly, joyfully, and with deliberation, have sacrificed everything for their children, knowing their children would not appreciate that love for many long years. It was an investment of faith: faith in what was right, and faith in their children.

Part of a father's sacrifice was sometimes, or maybe ofttimes, taking a stand, when they were not understood.

It could even seem that mothers undermined that sacrifice when they, driven by the strongest of maternal instinct, would soften the discipline a father decreed. Mom seemed fair, and dad remained unjust and uncaring. Was taking "a stand" worth that sacrifice?

The biggest early challenge in nearly every marriage is how to manage money. Two must blend very different

Being Consumed with Passion

approaches, and do the best they can, when the financial challenges come. And come they will.

The second biggest challenge in marriage endures well past that early financial negotiation. It is the challenge in how to discipline children.

God has enjoined us with strong, complementary perspectives on nearly everything. And few, if any, passions would exceed the passion devoted to children. But the balance couples find in their shared devotion will be one of the greatest blessings their children will unknowingly enjoy.

In some sense, this passion that consumed me was much like the often-misunderstood passion a father has for his children. I understood my father's strong passion better now than when I was young. That same strength was an example to me as I served these wonderful people. It was a consuming passion. Like my love for my family, it was so strong. Yet, with each passing day, it seemed to grow stronger still.

I loved these people. When they would suffer, I would suffer. It wasn't just sympathy. It was a divine empathy that suffered with them.

It was as though the Father's love was expressed in and through the Church. Christ loves us. He understood. He suffered for us. Somehow, He also suffered with us while on this earth. Our sins were borne by Him. He understood the grief of sin and our shame before God. This Man, that was God manifest in the flesh, was accursed of God for us. He died with the curse of sin upon Him, that we might live and die free from that curse. His curse was not earned; it was taken by grace. Our curse was earned; grace freed us.

It was that love that was consuming me. My passion was not indifferent; it grew. I was fully committed to this

Being Consumed with Passion

calling. Ava had said it; I echoed, "As much as any called to another land and a foreign people, I am called. I too am a missionary. This is my field. I am devoted with passion."

Ava and I shared this devotion. When we talked, I realized I was not alone. She was consumed as well. With the same maternal instinct she showed for our children, she would give herself to the care of this church.

This church could not understand the passion we had for them. I suppose that was the nature of how this worked. Much like a father whose love was misunderstood, and the love of the Father that cannot be understood, it was not their responsibility to understand. Parents, whose love is not understood, have no choice. Their hearts leave them no alternative. They will love their children. And so much more, our Father will love with a love that is absolute. It will not matter how much or little we know; it will not matter how much or how little we respond. Ava echoed what we had said many times before, "No, they can't understand the passion in our hearts. They don't realize how much passion we have for them." I answered, "I guess it isn't our job to ensure they understood. At least not yet. But it is our job to open our hearts, and let that passion consume us." The flame of the Holy Ghost would push us to His purpose being fulfilled in this city and, more certainly, in this people.

Being Consumed with Passion

READING GUIDE POINTS:
1. Passion is more determined than emotion
2. Your passion for your church will probably never be fully appreciated
3. Your passion for your church will sometimes be misunderstood
4. Passion grows with maturity
5. The longer you serve your church, the your more your passion for them will consume them
6. Passion compels sacrifice

References from:
Effective Christianity: Managing Life's Projects
- Chapter 9, page 88
  - There must be a total surrender to His purpose, and everything we have must be emptied
  - Total surrender does not hold back
- Chapter 11, page 102
  - Success comes to faithful people who trust that God will help them, believe success is ordained, will not accept failure, and will not stop until God's purposes are successfully accomplished

The Capacity for Mercy

I had heard teachers say, "To be a good teacher you have to be a good learner. The teacher must become a good role model to the students." It's easier", they said, "to follow someone who is a good example."

I wanted that to be true for me. More often than I wished, it seemed like my role as a teacher of God's Word was a contradiction.

I preached and taught about such things as repentance, revival, the Exodus, Psalms, miracles, the godhead, healing, temptation, forgiveness and sacrifice. The topics were many, and it sounded impressive. I was the voice of God in my teaching to this city. In the back of my mind, though, and sometimes front and center, I faced this contradiction. I asked myself how this could be.

I saw continually how little I still knew myself about these things, and yet it was my responsibility to teach them to others. I taught about repentance, and wondered if I knew how to repent myself. I taught of Moses in Exodus, and, at the same time, questioned my strength, my humility and my closeness to God. I needed to teach about sacrifice, but was I really an acceptable role model for sacrifice? I even felt some sense of shame when I was instructing others on dealing with temptation. It was a topic that, if we were honest, made all of us uncomfortable. I knew at least this – I could identify with the problem.

Then there was the matter of forgiveness. Even the most basic aspects of forgiveness weren't easy. Had I really forgiven myself? Had I really forgiven others? Did I truly understand forgiveness. I was learning more every day. So how could I teach it to others? It went beyond that. Forgiveness and reconciliation were coupled. I realized that reconciliation with others, and with God, was more than forgiveness. It was possible, even necessary, to forgive whether you understood someone or not. You could and must forgive someone even if they didn't acknowledge any wrong.

The Capacity for Mercy

That was really tough. Reconciliation, though, required more. To be reconciled meant understanding, having respect and many other things. Some form of communication and connection were necessary. I hadn't truly figured out forgiveness, and I certainly had a lot more to learn about reconciliation.

Mercy was added to that long list. I only had to compare my capacity for mercy to God's capacity for mercy, and I was driven to the altar. I was driven to the Bible to learn anew about one of the central issues of human life. I was driven to the Savior, my source of mercy, to seek and receive. Each time, I learned from He who embodied and exemplified mercy. Of all these contradictions that drove me to Him, there was one that, at least for a time, stood out. It was mercy.

Primed for His revelation, a simple family discussion would reveal the need further. Experience would pre-empt any Biblical study. And experience would seal understanding.

Ava had given of herself so selflessly. Daniel and Mia were committed. We were all drawn into this passion.

One day, at dinner, and after we had prayed for our church and our city, some things that had been building came out in the conversation. Children are honest, and at times blunt. When things seemed unfair, they would say so.

"It's not fair. Why must we always have a great attitude, when people don't appreciate us? We've sacrificed a lot, and they don't care. Why does it have to be us?"

It was very difficult to teach children about fairness. You insisted that they treat others fairly. At the same time, you needed to help them understand that life wasn't always fair. Fairness was an ideal that maturity tarnished. Their question was selfish, dangerous and understandable. We encouraged the children to keep doing the right thing, even when others didn't. We also encouraged them to do something very hard. We asked them to be fair about it, "No matter how badly you feel someone has hurt you, most of the time, they never intended to harm you." From their

The Capacity for Mercy

perspective that seemed impossible. I said to them, "The truth probably is that these people simply didn't think about what they were doing. As much as you feel it was about you, it probably wasn't. They never even considered for it would affect you." Seeing the total disbelief in their eyes, I told them, "An old pastor once said, 'Most people aren't against you; they're for themselves'." People meant to show appreciation. They knew it was right to do so. They would get so busy with their own lives. They failed to notice. If they had realized what they had done, they would have felt terrible. It may not have seemed possible, but the strong neglect that they felt was completely unintentional.

Later, privately, Ava shared that she sometimes felt the same way, "There are times when it seems like it is too much." Silently, I agreed. While encouraging the right spirit in our children, we faced the same battle ourselves. Our own self-pity empathized with our children. It seemed hard, but self-pity was dangerous and contagious.

Every leader could tell you that leadership was a lonely place. I was supposed to be the leader. I was called as a "man of God". But feelings wanted to take over. I had to be careful how I responded. Yes, I shared some of my wife's and my children's feelings. Whether justified or not, each of us had times when we felt neglected. Greatness was developed and revealed in difficult moments. Even how I responded to my family had to be guarded. I wanted someone to understand too.

We could not fall prey to bitterness. In doing so, we would begin to think of ourselves as victims, and 'they' would be the cause.

We could not demand that 'they owed us'. Instead of pleading on their behalf for mercy, we might have sought retribution for the way they had treated us. We could not be instruments of bitterness and vindication. Bitterness would have been a poison that derailed purpose. We had to determine to be instruments of His mercy.

The Capacity for Mercy

Contradiction had driven me to understand His mercy better. My need for this lesson was much greater than I realized. Only a merciful God could meet this need. I needed Him to open my eyes. And thankfully, He did.

God began to give me an awareness of things I had not understood. He opened my eyes to things I had not seen. This was not a lesson for others. Open to receive, and with a contradiction greater than I could have imagined, God began to teach me about mercy.

The first and now most obvious lesson was that mercy was more than a principle to be taught in a Bible study. It was more than an abstract theological concept. Mercy was real. It touched people. It was personal.

Another profound lesson was that all needed it. It was simple and central. Many have tried to ignore their own condition, but every person, when they have been honest, knows that they need mercy. If they had never acknowledged it, it was nonetheless true; they needed mercy.

I learned that mercy could not be controlled. It was not defined by a list of rules. Even on Mt. Sinai, at the very place of the giving of the law, God had proclaimed, "I will shew mercy on whom I will shew mercy (Ex. 33:19)." Man could never control it. It was never of merit, but in accordance with God's sovereignty (Ro 9:15-8).

Mercy was more expansive than I could grasp. God would choose mercy when I would not. That mercy was not reserved to a few, or a particular group. He was merciful to His creation. God has shown His mercy to all.

His covenant was coupled with His mercy, but mercy was not limited even by that covenant. His mercy has not been limited to only His chosen people. There were many lepers during the ministry of Elisha. Yet only the Syrian, Naaman, was healed (II Ki 5). During great famine, it was a Lebanese (Sidonian) woman, a widow of Zarephath, that was sustained with Elijah (I Ki 17). The Jews

The Capacity for Mercy

were driven to wrath by Jesus at the Mt of Precipice when He reminded them of these historical facts (Lu 4).

He revealed to me that mercy was more than salvation. One morning, Ava and I had a conversation about how both of us were learning about mercy. I said, "I used to think of mercy only in the context of people being saved. This has taught me that mercy is much more than that. God is merciful to unsaved people as well." "You know," she said, "I hadn't thought of it that way either. Hearing you say that, though, it's obviously true." Mercy was unearned; it was bestowed through compassion. Compassion, and its resultant mercy, was not defined or limited by any status, even salvation.

If I was to be consumed with passion, I also needed to be consumed with mercy. My striving was to align my understanding and my actions with His mercy. Truthfully, these great lessons only strengthened my confession, "God, I thought I understood this. Now, I confess that I don't see your mercy the way you do. I need to grow in my understanding. I see now that your determined mercy is to all."

If God was to be my example, how was I supposed to bestow mercy? Unable to grasp it in its entirety, His voice and the passion He had put in my soul compelled me to do better. I had to be a caring, merciful neighbor. Like the story of the Good Samaritan, openly I needed to ask, "Who is my neighbor?"

Mercy was no longer something I would only seek for myself. I would seek and plead for His mercy for others. I would plead that God would be merciful to this city and our nation. The need for mercy was universal.

I would be patient and seek God's mercy for those slow to respond. I would still seek God's mercy for those who rejected the truth. It would not be my place to decide who would be granted mercy. I would now want everyone to have mercy. No, they didn't deserve it. Starkly, I recognized that I didn't deserve it either.

Mercy was harnessed with purpose. I would act with

The Capacity for Mercy

purpose to extend His mercy to the fullest. I would be thankful for every positive response, and for each small step. My new goal was to let thankfulness abide in me.

There would be focus and expansion. We would start with those where there was common ground. So, we would start with those we could connect with most easily. It would be much like establishing a customer profile in a marketing plan. We would establish an initial "beachhead". We would be intentional, but not exclusive. First, we had to start. The goal was for His mercy to reach all.

READING GUIDE POINTS:
1. We will never fully understand God's capacity for mercy
2. Jesus embodied and exemplified mercy
3. It is mercy that compels us to expand our own capacity for mercy
4. Mercy does not demand fairness
5. Mercy is more than a principle; it is real
6. Everyone needs mercy
7. We do not control mercy
8. Mercy is more than salvation
9. We should seek God's mercy for everyone
10. Mercy is coupled with purpose

References from:
Effective Christianity: Managing Life's Projects
- Chapter 3, page 22
  - We are to show compassion on any one who is in need
  - Each need requires someone to care and act, and that requires a compassionate person of the Spirit to set a goal to change things

The Trajectory of Responsibility

This story could have been told from either a male or female perspective. Both apply. Edwin and I discussed it, and thought it might be best to tell this from a woman's point of view.

As a young girl, I didn't dream of being famous or strong and courageous. I didn't need to conquer anything or be a great hero. That was for boys. There was no driving ambition to set my own course necessarily, although a few of my friends had some of those ambitions. I enjoyed being a girl. At a young age, I made my dream clear, "I want to be a lady, and be treated like one."

Some of my dreams echoed that desire. I dreamed of marriage and what it would be like. What kind of person would my husband be? It wasn't about how he looked, or how handsome he would be. Just being a great husband would make him handsome to me. I dreamed of the attention and special feelings I would have when he proposed, and how special my wedding would be.

I dreamed of going to beautiful or romantic places. Places like Hawaii, Vienna, or the Eiffel Tower were on that list. I didn't have any desire to be a doctor or president, but I did dream of having a successful career, and I wanted to be a great mom.

There came a time, though, for independence. No longer a wistful little girl, there were other things demanding my attention. I remembered moving into my first apartment. Of course, my parents wanted to be sure I was ready. I told them why it was so important to me, "It isn't just to prove to you I can do it. I need to prove it to myself. And I don't want

The Trajectory of Responsibility

to be in a position where I'm desperate to find a husband because I can't take care of myself. I need this confidence."

I wasn't making a lot of money, but I had a decent job. I had already told mom and dad that I was thinking of moving. Mom commented, "Ava, I'm still not sure I like this idea." Both she and dad made sure that I had looked at the numbers, and that I could afford it.

I was pretty sure I could do it, and made the move. I soon discovered things were more expensive than I thought. There were things I hadn't considered. And I had to make some choices. That meant going without some things.

One day, I was visiting mom and dad, and I asked a simple question, "Do you know how much it costs for shampoo?"

The response surprised me. Mom started to laugh. Then she couldn't stop. She laughed so hard there were tears in her eyes. She looked at my puzzled expression through those tears, and came close. She put her arms around me. I still hadn't figured out how the question was so funny. "My dear Ava, I'm sorry. I wasn't expecting that. Yes, dear, we do know. We have paid for a lot of shampoo. When you were living at home, we asked you the same question many times." Dad was observing with a composed smile. Then with a love that fathers have for their daughters, Dad also reminded me, "You didn't understand then, and you wouldn't listen. We tried to tell you. Do you remember all of those times I said, 'As long as you're living in my house.' Well, this was a part of it. You had to have these expensive things. You had to have your way. We were trying to do our best, but it wasn't easy. Now, you understand for yourself."

The Trajectory of Responsibility

I was doing my best. As much as I wanted complete independence, mom and dad would help once in a while. If something broke or needed maintenance, dad would help me out. I would meet mom for lunch sometimes. She would always say, "Oh, let me take care of that," when the bill for our meal came. I found out later that dad would ask if she intended to help, and then give her money. If we went somewhere, they would pay for the gasoline. Both of them would say, "We never want to be a financial burden to you."

We would go to mom and dad's house to celebrate dad's birthday. Mom would cook. Then one year, I took the big step. I told mom first, "I want you and dad to come over to my place to celebrate dad's birthday. I'll do something simple." Mom said, "Ava, your father will love that." Then she insisted, "You must let me bring something." I couldn't say no, but I had taken this step.

Dad said that was all he needed for a birthday present. "All I want is to spend time with you, and be proud of what you have become. I love you as much as I did when you were a little girl. Ava, I'm so proud of you. My love for you isn't any less. Fathers don't need reasons, but you give me plenty of reasons to be proud." I could tell he really meant it. He was really proud of me. It was dad's birthday, but I got the best present, dad's praise.

Edwin's story was similar. Really, neither his story or mine was unique. In fact, it was the same story each church planter could tell. Every child went through three simple phases. They were totally dependent; there was a transition toward independence; they became independent.

It was much like moving into my first apartment. At the beginning, it was important, to take advantage of every

The Trajectory of Responsibility

opportunity to learn and benefit from other people. Edwin and I needed others. We needed their help. We needed to hear their stories. Independence didn't mean learning and doing everything by ourselves. Honestly, we would never stop learning from others. Without them, I don't see how we would have survived. I had heard people say, "I got here all by myself. I didn't need help from anyone else." It wasn't that way for us. Easily, we kept a spirit of appreciation. From start to finish, we would acknowledge the contribution and investment of others.

There would come a transition where we could begin to take ownership. We consciously planned for that phase, but it wouldn't come easily, and it often seemed that it wasn't early enough. We were trying to do our best, and often it was a struggle, "We want to be responsible. We don't want to be a burden on others any longer than necessary. Taking responsibility, though, will require determination."

This transition phase left us vulnerable. We were in the process of separating from our 'safety net'. Fortunately, mature, seasoned leaders understood this vulnerability.

We had a meeting with our old pastor and his wife. They insisted on paying for the meal. They knew what we were going through, and the choices it required. There was an assurance that calmed us. The pastor said, "There are many in the church have given us so many reasons to be proud as their pastor. It's not just a few, but many have made it all rewarding." And he added, "I can't think of any reason for us to be more proud than to see a wonderful couple like you two answering the call of God, and following in our footsteps in planting a church." Our pastor's wife beamed as the godly example she had always been to the mothers in our

The Trajectory of Responsibility

church. She gripped my hand, and said she was so proud as well, "I see how you have grown. Seeing you live for the Lord is all we could ask for." The pastor then said, "We expect nothing from you." I remembered my dad when the pastor said that it was enough to join with us, and rejoice with us in seeing God's will unfold. "We pray one day you will have the same opportunity to spend time with another young couple, and understand what we feel in our hearts today." Once again, our pastor was speaking for the Lord. God's voice was clear through his. He wasn't rebuking or demanding anything, but somehow as he said that, we knew that it was also part of our calling to reproduce a similar vision in others.

This trajectory of responsibility was much like being a teenager desperately wanting to show independence. There was strong desire and determination. We couldn't be premature though. We couldn't proclaim that we were completely independent too soon. There was a period where we felt alone as we had to determine for ourselves when we could take complete responsibility. Others would help as we needed it, but wouldn't decide for us when the transition was over. The loneliness of that decision was sometimes troubling.

Independence was, in some ways, a contradiction. Especially in spiritual matters, independence was never absolute. It was about taking ownership, not about isolation. We would still need good friends and good counsel.

Eventually, though, we would be comfortable with our personal responsibility. The day did come. We were no longer financially dependent on those dear friends who helped us. Those closest and most devoted to our growth were not obstructive or critical. They were not offended by our need or

The Trajectory of Responsibility

our eventual independence either. Edwin and I would ever appreciate their role and their example. Like parents, they were proud of our growth and maturity. We had given them reason to be proud of their support. One dear friend said, "We have immense satisfaction in seeing that you are now established, able to take care of yourselves, and able to start helping others." That important lesson we believe, one day, we will pass on as well.

READING GUIDE POINTS:
1. Responsibility drives us to not be dependent on others
2. Taking personal responsibility is usually a transition process
3. Caring people will help you in your transition to independence
4. Complete independence, especially spiritual independence, is a contradiction
5. We never outgrow appreciation
6. Establishing independence reveals vulnerability
7. Instill responsibility in others

References from:
Effective Christianity: Managing Life's Projects

- Chapter 4, page 31
  - We know that we have been called by the Spirit to a higher calling and a new, eternal purpose. Our new lives are anointed for that purpose.
- Chapter 4, page 32
  - When you are exposed to God's vision, burden comes with it
- Chapter 4, page 33
  - We are willing to do whatever He asks us to do
- Chapter 4, page 34
  - We must know when it is our responsibility to respond
- Chapter 4, page 37
  - If you're going to seek, find and fulfill His will, you must respond when He reveals that will. Response requires action.
  - To accomplish your purpose, you must take some risk
  - Fulfilling God's will is not about personal satisfaction; it is about the balance between submission and responsibility.
- Chapter 4, page 38
  - Dreams themselves do not produce results; actions do
- Chapter 4, page 39
  - If we take action when He leads us, we will know the joy of seeing His will and our greatest dreams fulfilled
- Chapter 4, page 42
  - If we are steadfast in our pursuit of ministerial excellence, the church becomes the refuge that the true church is destined to be
- Chapter 4, page 43
  - We must be spiritually effective. Much is at stake. Our effectiveness matters.

Fitly Framed

I felt so overwhelmed. In my mind, I knew better. Faith demanded that I trust the Lord. This faith, this trust, was what I proclaimed to others. Yet in my heart, it was different. I had said many times when counseling others going through difficulty, "Trust in the Lord.". Now it was my turn.

I was overwhelmed with all of the things I needed to be. There were too many roles it was my job to play. I needed to be an evangelist and a soul-winner. I needed to have an outgoing personality. My roles included being a delegator, doer, visionary, missionary, planner, coordinator, administrator, and a financial manager. I was supposed to be the risk taker and, at the same time, the risk manager. I was a project manager and a teacher. I was the preacher, but I also had to be the learner. I rehearsed the terrifying list too many times. I just couldn't be all of those things, and I certainly couldn't be all of the at the same time.

I found it wasn't just me. Ava had troubling moments that were expressed this way, "I feel like I have to be a perfect example. That's an impossible challenge. We have real children. They aren't role models on some display for their perfection. They are still children." They, Ava and I all had our weaknesses and flaws. Where were these perfect people who could do all of these things? We couldn't measure up to this level of greatness. How were we possibly fit for this?

For a time that seemed longer than it actually was, a storm was looming in my heart. I was trying to trust that He had called me, knowing my gifts and my deficiencies. Yes, I would be strong. Yes, I believed in His call. Yes, I would trust

Fitly Framed

Him. I breathed more easily, knowing the battle in my heart was now over. Then the list would be rehearsed again, and the looming storm would return.

The Lord did bring peace. It was not a powerful sense of anointing and confidence. It wasn't the strength of my will winning over the weakness in my heart. It came as a simple, assuring memory.

While I was troubled about all that needed to be done, the Lord showed me a lesson. It was something I had seen, but hadn't yet appreciated until the Lord opened my eyes. The lesson had been taught many years ago. While I was worrying about all of the roles that needed to be filled in our church, I was reminded of an elderly man in our old church.

An elderly saint sat in the back of our old church. In his youth, he no doubt was active, participating in church activities. Time had taken its demands on him physically. He wasn't the active young man he used to be.

He still had a role in the Kingdom though. For anyone lucky or wise enough to chat with him, they would receive encouragement. Time had taken its toll physically, but in his spirit, he was strong. It would have been easy, seeing his struggle, to complain and be critical. To the contrary, he chose to only be encouraging. When you spoke to him, there would be no rebuke. There were no orders about how you should behave though we gave him ample ammunition for such admonition. He would always say something positive. And you were always special. They would hear, "You're doing a great job. I have confidence in you. You've got a good heart. I know you'll do the right thing." He didn't go to them; people would come to him. They wanted just to sit and talk with him.

I didn't see him for a while. By the time I missed him,

Fitly Framed

there was a prayer request. His health was failing. Sadly, he died in only a few days.

I decided to attend the funeral. He didn't hold any position in the church. He wasn't participating in any sanctioned church activities. I wanted to get there early. Walking out the door, I remember saying, "There probably won't be many people there." As I approached the church, I was surprised at first. The parking lot was full. I wondered if something else was going on too. Maybe since it would be such a small funeral, the church decided they could have another event at the same time.

What happened next was an even bigger surprise. When I got to the front door of the church, the line for visitation was backed up to the door. I had to wait a long time to pay well-earned respect for him and offer my comfort to the family. I was glad I had gotten there early, but for reasons opposite to what I expected. The funeral service started late because so many people were in line for the viewing. After the ceremony, the pastor said, "This was one of the most well-attended funerals we ever had."

Through this memory, the Lord made application to the lesson He had given many years ago. I was so worried about all of the positions that had to be filled. I was burdened trying to see that every role was performed. The Lord showed me that He can fill roles I don't even imagine. He had placed people as He saw fit, and their value to the Kingdom was great. During the funeral, one of the speakers had said, "This great saint had no recognized position in OUR church. He did, though, have a great position in THE church." He was fitly framed by the Master.

There was a new confidence. It was now well-placed.

Fitly Framed

Our church would be fitly framed. We would not be able to orchestrate all of the skills, talents or personalities that would make the church successful. God would fitly frame all of those things Himself. God was leading others to us, knowing their gifts and their deficiencies. He would bring the right people and blend them into His body. That balance would bring strength of a frame fitted perfectly.

I recognized my own calling. Now He was calling me to another recognition, "Trust in my calling of others just as strongly as you trust in my calling of you."

My responsibility as a father and my passion for my children demonstrated I could. I remember when each of my children was born. Their development amazed me. I inherently believed in them. I knew God would use them mightily. It was easy (well, sometimes) to believe in my own calling. It was natural to believe in the potential of my children. The Lord was challenging me to believe in His calling in others as strongly as I did in myself and my children.

I was also drawn to many portions of Scripture that exemplified this truth.

I Corinthians 12 wasn't only about specific gifts and offices. There were fundamental principles revealed. Identifying and defining each gift and office was important. The simple, compelling example of the human body showed there was a more collective principle. God had "set every one of them in the body, as it hath pleased Him" (I Co 12:18). This simple principle was that the gifts of one are as important as the gifts of another (I Co 12:24-25).

I had studied the book of Ephesians, with its theme of unity in the church. Ephesians 4 said much about unity: one body, one Lord, one faith, and one baptism. The Gospel and

Fitly Framed

salvation were the same for all. And the ministries listed in Eph 4:11 were for the "unity of the faith" Prior to those points in chapter 4, however, Paul established another foundational divine concept: "We are all fitly framed together" (Eph 2:21).

The building of the Temple served as another example. David had prepared for the building that would follow him. Every piece was completed before the Temple was built by Solomon. Each piece was made to fit before it was set in place. It was all according to God's divine plan.

God fitly framed each piece. They didn't have to make these pieces work. He established importance and purpose of each of them. If any piece had not fit, the integrity of the Temple would have been compromised.

While the abundance of gold and silver was astonishing, every stone was also important. The building's strength wasn't in the pieces thought most valuable; it was in the stable, unadorned pieces that didn't get much attention.

It was one year until our planned launch. With this fresh awareness of each person's value, I asked the Lord, "How do you want me to build this team? I feel like a coach, wanting to make the best of each team member." If there was to be strategy, it was to build on this team. Fulfilling God's will in each of their lives was part of my responsibility. It wasn't just about the goals the Lord had put in my heart. I had a burden for them as well. Further, this awareness meant that their development was just as important as mine.

Where would we start? God would finish the work in His way, but we still had to do our part. What were our choices? How would I manage these precious resources, and follow the leading of the Holy Ghost? The first step was the

Fitly Framed

most obvious. I would start with the people I knew: my family, and friends that we knew. Then I would look for people that were capable, and see how God could use those capabilities. I trusted that people would rise to the challenge. God was leading me to challenge them well. Some of those people would have capabilities and potential that had been overlooked in the past. If I used my own judgment, I would likely overlook someone with great potential, that had a calling on their lives.

Doing my part included building a plan. The plan needed to answer three questions:

What teams would we need?

What gifts would be suited best for each team?

When would each team be needed?

I told Ava how I felt the Lord has answered those questions, "I've decided on three teams, a launch team, a core team, and volunteer staff. Regarding gifts, I recognize that some will be a better fit for one team than another. I want each person to be on a team that will allow them to focus on their gifts." And how will we know when each team is needed?", Ava asked. "I don't know what else to do but build a schedule, and make sure these things are in the first-year plan."

Lastly, and most importantly, we would discover how God builds His church. It was our job to do our best. We would plan as well as we could. Our motto was to have plans, but not to put our trust in those plans.

As we were preparing to build these teams, God gave us new examples of how He works beyond our means.

A man who was a new convert wanted to help. He wasn't interested in any position. He didn't really want to join a team. But he could do simple things. He asked, "Can I help

Fitly Framed

by mowing the grass?" We certainly needed someone to help with that. It was something that was in his heart. It's the one way he knew he could help. It reminded me of the elderly saint in our old church who did what he could do. He too didn't ask for attention, but made a big difference connecting with and encouraging people. This was another role, but we would see how it would bloom.

After a few weeks, and with no attention on my part, I noticed flowers were planted at the church entrance. There were also fresh flowers in vases on the steps at the doorway. I asked the man helping mow the grass if he knew who was doing this. He said, "Oh, yeah. Another couple asked me if they could help with flowers. I didn't think about it. It seemed like a great idea. I hope you don't mind, pastor, but I told them it was fine with me. Knowing how thankful you were, I didn't think there would be a problem." There was no need for coordination. This man's devotion to his gifts triggered something in them too. There was no expectation or desire for recognition.

I could take no credit for it. We had been very busy. There were many things on our list, but we hadn't had the capacity to put this in our plans. It made our church look so welcoming, and it made a difference. Many visitors commented, "Oh, your church looks so nice and welcoming. The flowers are beautiful."

After doing all that we could, God reminded us that this was His church. It was His plan to build this church in this city. We learned again that only He could fit each of our personalities, skills, and calling to devotion to His eternal purpose. As it was with the ancient church in Ephesus, each team and each person would be 'fitly framed' in His kingdom.

Fitly Framed

> **READING GUIDE POINTS:**
> 1. Each member of the body is important
> 2. Calling requires us to not only recognize our own gifts and calling, but to recognize the gifts and callings in others
> 3. God will provide the balance of gifts your church needs
> 4. God will orchestrate His purpose for your church beyond your means
> 5. Always remember it is His church

> **References from:**
> ***Effective Christianity: Managing Life's Projects***
> - Chapter 9, page 83
>   - The purpose of resource management is to make the most effective use of all project resources
>   - An important objective is to spiritually strengthen those involved
> - Chapter 9, page 84
>   - In spite of your weakness, your talent is sufficient in His hands
> - Chapter 9, page 85
>   - There must be faith that God can be successful through you
> - Chapter 9, page 87
>   - Our God, the Master of all things, and the Manager of heaven and all things temporal and eternal, can take those that are least significant, and develop them to great success
> - Chapter 9, page 88
>   - When assessed fully, there is faith that the needed people, material and funding will be obtained

Connecting (the Lost)

A good friend of our family had recently passed away. Death was one of those things we eventually couldn't ignore. Sometimes it would force its way into our lives. Ava and I both knew this friend. After the funeral, we thought about it a lot for a while.

"I'm concerned for the family, dear", I said to Ava. "My heart grieves for them. I can't imagine what they're going through with this loss. And honestly, I don't want to imagine it. It would be like me losing you."

"What about us?", she asked. "Are we taking care of ourselves as we should? Should we make some changes? Should we get more exercise? What do we have to give up to create time for other things?"

"I don't talk about it much, but I don't like to imagine it either. Sometimes I try to imagine how I would cope if I lost you, and then I have to stop thinking about it, because it's just too hard."

Sometimes, people had no choice. It would have been very hard dealing with the loss of a loved one. It seemed that there were more widows than widowers, so wives were the ones more likely dealing with loss. Helping others deal with loss was part of our duty in the ministry. Many times, Ava and I were with a grieving widow, and this was how the conversation would go:

"I can't imagine life without my husband. Being together is all I've known for many years. His companionship was part of me. I could depend on him being there whenever I needed him. Our companionship was a stable rock, a foundation shared joyfully every day. And now it's gone."

Connecting (the Lost)

There were always profound questions that only time could answer:

"How do I go on living?"
"Will I ever be able to laugh again?"
"Can this sorrow pass?"
"How do I just dismiss who he was?"

It wasn't really our responsibility to answer the questions. Often in trials, we had found that understanding the questions was more important than having answers. It was our responsibility to comfort as we could, and help them focus on He who had eternal answers.

It rarely ended there. The children couldn't fathom how to not have a father. They couldn't reconcile God, fairness and death. But in those moments, who could? They would say, "Life isn't fair. Why did God take my father? My friends sill have their dads. Why don't I?" For them as well, their father was a rock in their lives that they could trust. That strength that they trusted had been ripped away. Their grief was no less profound.

Children were resilient, though, or at least appeared to be. They could usually occupy themselves, being busy with other families and friends. That would help distract and comfort them. But the deep, underlying loss was still there. It would resurface, seldom in their words, more often in their behavior. Sensitivity, compassion and connection were paramount if you were to help.

Their sorrow was cruel and stark. Always, it would painfully remind those affected that death and eternity were real. This reality drove the church in its mission to save the lost. To the lost there was a message. "Don't wait. Yes, death and eternity are real. Please respond now!"

To the lost, I offered a loving warning that seemed dire. But I also offered them an opportunity for peace. For surely, there was peace in the death of someone saved. Loss sought comfort. I could encourage them confidently, "Knowing they are in heaven is the greatest comfort. Their suffering is over. Eternal beauty and joy is their new reality, and it will be unending." Through all of their grief, we could say assuredly that it was the one thing that would help them to carry on. It was what living for the Lord was all about.

The final human reality of death and the eternal reality that followed compelled me to heed the universal commission to "go ye into all the world, and preach the gospel to every creature." I had to reach the lost. I believed what the church proclaimed was real. I believed what the church proclaimed was the answer, and that our church needed to take the Great Commission seriously. We needed to reach everyone in our city. My passion to connect with the lost was driven by three key beliefs.

I believed in Heaven. Otherwise, I wouldn't have been there. The reason I was there was to change the eternal destiny of the people of this city. Helping people get to heaven was what drove me.

I believed in Hell. Eternity was a reality. Every person would either go to Heaven or go to Hell. There was consequence to how people lived their lives. Faith did matter. I was convinced of that. That conviction was of ultimate importance. It was the most important matter in this life.

I believed that the Gospel would save the lost. What I was doing wasn't just a vocation. What I was doing was of eternal importance. I had to win the lost. One day, Ava said,

Connecting (the Lost)

"These people won't just be our friends; we are going to heaven together." How true that was. The fellowship we had was part of the eternal life we would enjoy together. I concurred, saying, "We can't lose sight of heaven. It's what we're hoping for. It's what the lost need."

Connecting with the lost, then, could not be something haphazard. Connection would not happen by accident; it had to be intentional. Certainly, Ava and I and our developing church had all been doing our best already to connect with our community. But that was more about our attitude towards connecting and creating general awareness. Now we needed a plan to connect with lost souls in our city. As with so many other things, there was an important administrative or practical component to this sobering spiritual mandate. We had to be effective, in connecting, and in saving the lost.

There were three fundamental elements of the plan. The first element was to define who we would connect with intentionally. A mentor has said: "Start with categories of knowing: people you already know, people you would like to know, and people you used to know." That advice sounded pretty basic, but it turned out to be a good starting point. It also forced us to do something hard to do: choose. We needed and wanted to reach every soul in our city. Why would we exclude anyone from the plan? Our mentor had encouraged us that to be effective in our outreach there had to be focus. Having a plan required choices to be made. This is where we would start.

The second element was how we would communicate. We rehearsed our 'elevator speech' repeatedly. As it was to connect with the community in general, so it would be to connect with lost souls. Daniel had told me about elevator

Connecting (the Lost)

speeches. I told him, "We have to be intentional about having conversations, and we have to be prepared with what we will say." "Sure", he said. "That's kind of what an elevator speech is all about."

But being prepared to speak was only part of it. Again, our mentors' advice was so helpful. One mentor said it this way, "Learn how to listen. Learn to listen before speaking. People don't want to be told what to do; they want people to listen."

The third element was having a clear understanding of what was necessary for our connecting to be successful. There would have to be purpose in connecting. We wanted souls to be saved. We would focus our attention on people interested in spiritual change. As strange as it seemed, the truth was that not everyone wanted spiritual change. They may have been complacent, indifferent, or spiritually defiant, but some would be uninterested. Yes, everyone was important, but we had to focus our attention and devote our limited time to those that showed interest.

Success would also require determination. We had to have a mindset of continual sowing. Again, it wasn't just for me and Ava. We rehearsed it to our church, "It has to become a natural part of our personal and collective conversations. We will never get to a place where we can stop reaching for the lost. There will always be more lost people with whom we could connect. Each of them will be different. Each one will be a person with identity. Effective determination will require that we persist and adapt."

Connecting (the Lost)

READING GUIDE POINTS:
1. You must believe that what the Church proclaims is the answer
2. Your church must take the Great Commission seriously
3. You must believe in heaven
4. You must believe in hell
5. You must believe that the Gospel will save the lost
6. Intentionally define with whom you will connect
7. Intentionally define how you will communicate with the lost
8. You must connect with purpose; define what makes communication successful
9. Connecting effectively requires persistence and adaptation

References from:
Effective Christianity: Managing Life's Projects
- Chapter 5, page 44
    - Set goals
- Chapter 5, page 45
    - Build unity of purpose with goals that all can see
    - Develop a plan
    - Chapter 5, page 49
        - Evaluate how effective you are
            - What should you do to improve?
            - Share what you are doing; get them involved too
    - We do need to know if the job is getting done. Performance means we are accomplishing our intended results.

What They Need

"Today, I feel well." That was the thought capturing my attention only a few days after panic nearly consumed me. The panic I had felt a few days ago had been replaced. Yes, the teaching plan made me feel better. But it wasn't just the plan that resulted from my panic. There was something more. I tried to avoid the roller coasters of emotion. I knew emotion could be a dangerous, unstable motivator. But there was a new confidence that I couldn't explain. I asked myself, "What changed? Before I said I was sick in my soul. Now, in my soul, I feel strong." I knew faith had taken over. It was a renewed faith that made me feel stronger.

To some, this story must have seemed strange. Ava and I knew that, and we talked about it. She had said many times, "It probably seems like there are so many things that would make others think that this is only negative. Sure, there has been plenty of struggle. I don't think that will stop. Yes, the maturity being placed upon us is enormous. There haven't been many days lately where we could relax. Each day, there are so many things to do, there are battles every day, and the spiritual warfare seems unending." To many, that would have sounded like a bitter complaint.

But, perhaps surprisingly, neither Ava nor I were negative at all. To her, I had said, "Sure, we could allow these things to make us feel negative. We could complain that so many things are unfair. More than that, we could even become bitter, and think that God has forsaken us, in leading us to a place, away from the security we knew, to a position where everything is difficult." Easily, that could have been the feeling. We could have justified those feelings. If the stories

What They Need

that we had told led people to that understanding, though, it was a mistaken understanding.

No, and to the contrary, we were happy. There was no bitterness. We were not dejected, or pitying ourselves. In the midst of that struggle and tested growth there was certainty and continuing, growing passion. Instead of complaint or pity, for each of us the testimony was, "I have no regret. The journey is rewarding. I wouldn't trade it for anything."

I had been saying that, "I can't explain it. Something has changed. Something has given us confidence in the midst of our struggle. What is it?" In asking, things that were evident emerged from our wonder.

The same convictions were renewed. They were not new. They had not changed. The convictions of truth and calling were unabated. Renewed conviction beckoned us to renewed confidence. But there was one thing, and only one thing that had changed. We began to see our purpose in a new light.

Though shared, conviction was not communal. It was and had to be personal. A message arose that I penned, "I believe in this truth. With absolute confidence, I truly believe in the message of Christ: His birth, His life, His death, His burial, His resurrection, His ascension, His promise, His presence, His comfort, His assurance, His love. The magnitude of His greatness is beyond my expression and my comprehension. When I begin to recount all of those things, there is no end to why I believe in Jesus."

I believed in His calling. This conviction had been often tested, but had not wavered. He had called Ava and me to be where we were. He was calling others in this city. He was calling for a church in this city. It was all part of His

What They Need

predestined plan. If so, then in a real sense, my calling was of eternal purpose, and the gates of hell would not prevail against it. That was my conviction. Struggle or not, we were doing what we were supposed to do; we were where we were supposed to be.

In the steadfastness of conviction, my purpose was renewed in a new light. It was about more than my responsibility. Need and opportunity merged. The need of the lost was more than a burden in my heart. Their need gave me confidence. Inspiration said, "The church has what they need."

I knew that. I was firmly convinced of it. But it needed to be solidified. Were there specific things I could identify that they needed? Said differently, "What is it that they don't have and will find in the church?" The list could have been longer, but I came up with five things.

They needed repentance. It seemed so basic. Repentance was a universal need, and it was found in the church. It was not to the church that they would repent, but it would be in the church that they would be drawn to a place of repentance. They would be drawn to Christ, to whom they could repent and find forgiveness. They needed to know this simple truth, "In this church you will find the repentance you seek. You will find what you need."

They needed baptism. They needed to identify completely with Him. At the start, baptism to most was a step of obedience, but in time, they would recognize the value and necessity of it as identity. Baptism, though, was more than a necessary ritual. With it was an essential experience. We could say, "Here, you will experience the cleansing that

What They Need

comes as you are covered in the water of baptism. In this church, your need will be met."

They needed to be filled with His Spirit. The infilling of the Holy Spirit is transcendent and transforming. They needed to know that indescribable feeling that comes when He fills them with His Spirit. They needed the assurance that His indwelling Spirit would bring when troubles would come. They needed that abiding joy that would be with them in every good moment, and yes, through every trial as well. Still, we could say, "In this church, you will find the divine infilling you need."

They needed to have a new life in Him. They needed to know what it was like to walk with the Lord every day, and to have His presence with them in every moment. They need to have and to know the peace, joy, promise, and assurance that is the essence of a new life in Christ. They need to commit their lives to spiritual growth and maturity, and know the reward of that great life. They needed to have eternal life. With certainty, we could say, "The eternal life you can know in your present, human journey can be found in this church."

They needed hope. There is a hope that only He can bring, and they needed to know it. Their lives would have moments of sadness and disappointment, but in Him, those moments would be eclipsed by that hope, and they needed to know that. They needed to have and to know a hope that would not be taken away. They needed a hope that was true. Of that, we could say, "In this church, you will find that hope."

They needed fellowship. They needed a church that would provide a personal touch in their lives, and we were determined to be that kind of church. The needed the

What They Need

fellowship that this church would provide. They needed to fellowship with people who knew what it was like to have His indwelling Spirit. Then they, for themselves, with like people, would share this experience that could not be explained. Yet, they too would know, because they had experienced it themselves. Our promise was this, "In this church, you will have personal fellowship with people who will share your joys, sorrows, and testimony."

Yes, I felt well. With renewed and emboldened confidence, I could say, "This church HAS what you need. This church IS what you need." As part of our calling and the calling of all who would be a part of it, this church would be a foundation for their rewarding, productive, spiritual growth.

I could see even beyond their current needs. I wasn't just about their maturity. Yes, they needed to grow. They needed to be witnesses, teachers, and preachers. More than that, they needed to reproduce, to bring other, new souls into the kingdom. They would be new missionaries, and carry the truth themselves.

Yes, we had what they needed. But it was more than "selling the message" to a target market. Certainly, the message had to be communicated effectively. But their need was more than an end to our goals and profit. They were not, and we would not treat them, as a means to our personal end. The message was this, "These people are souls, destined to His kingdom, and this is what their souls need. They need Jesus. They need to be saved." I was convinced; we had what they needed.

Practically, then, how would they find what they needed? How would we be effective in merging their need and our opportunity? How did we need to think to see that

What They Need

souls in need would find what they needed in this church?

We would focus on cooperation and recognition. That focus was part of being 'fitly framed'. We would use everyone that was willing to participate. We would recognize each gift. The concept of diversity had been corrupted by the world. There was, though, a divine concept of diversity. We would embrace God's definition. Rather than competitors, our values said, "Each member is just as important as the next. No one is better or worse. We will win, and we will win together."

Effectiveness required there be vision and structure for growth. We would unite in a vision of a growing church, and an effective church in this city. We understand the need for effective administration. I wanted it to be clear, "Administration is the cement that supports everything else. We will do our best to be structured, but not bureaucratic. We need structure, but structure by itself, will save no one."

Effective planning would include tools for growth. Growth was not simply an organic inevitability. It would be intentional. It would be planned. There would be tools to support it.

In all of these well-intentioned efforts, I would also be thankful for those who had paved the way before me. Ava told me something she had discovered through some of the online materials, "Before there was a planter, someone watered. Someone prepared the soil, not just for harvest, but first, for planting." That was so true. Others had seen the vision and had prepared the way, not yet seeing the harvest themselves.

I wanted Daniel and Mia to know they were not alone. I also wanted them to know that, in spite of our sacrifice, we

What They Need

had not done this by ourselves. At the supper table one night, I told them, "Yes, we are the church planters, but we could only plant where there was soil that was ready. I now understand their courage and sacrifice. We should always honor them as a foundation set before us."

This, then, was my joyful calling. It was not a calling of sorrow. It was the Lord that gave me strength, hope, and confidence. I knew we had what this city needed. I knew that what I was doing was right. It was what I wanted to do.

READING GUIDE POINTS:
1. In the midst of your struggle, there is still peace
2. True conviction and calling are not dissuaded by struggle
3. The lost need repentance
4. The lost need baptism
5. The lost need to be filled with the Spirit
6. The lost need hope
7. The lost need fellowship of the Church
8. The lost need to become mature, productive disciples
9. Our focus must not be on what we want, but on what their souls need
10. Each member of the body is fitly framed to meet the needs of the lost
11. Connecting effectively requires vision, structure, and intentional, effective planning and tools

What They Need

> **References from:**
> ***Effective Christianity: Managing Life's Projects***
> - Chapter 3, page 23
>   - We are called to help those in need. We must strive to be effective in doing so
> - Chapter 3, page 24
>   - Everyone's gifts and calling are unique.
> - Chapter 3, page 29
>   - To be effective in your calling and in meeting their need, you must blend being spiritual and practical
> - Chapter 7, pages 70-75
>   - When your calling is certain and your vision is clear, you are then able to recognize and know that vision, to communicate it to others, and to persevere.

The Call from the Hungry

I had heard people say, "The concept of calling itself is simple." I knew, though, that those words weren't true. There was so much depth to it that the term 'simple' was too trivial. Calling was meaningful and driven with purpose. Others had said, "Each saved person has a call of God on their lives." Yes, that was true, but it was also true to say, "Only those who have a call can understand it." They key was recognizing and accepting that call. Only those not yet committed to it would dare call it simple. It wasn't until someone accepted the call of God that they really began to understand what the call of God was, and specifically, what their calling was.

Most of the time, when people talked about the call of God, they talked about it in the sense of TO. It seemed it was in one direction. They talked about what they were called TO, "I am called TO [a city]. I am called TO [a people]." People in this city were even called TO this church. They were called TO connect with us. This call TO things was like a push from the Lord TO them and TO us.

As people matured in understanding the call of God and their specific calling, though, they realized that the calling had two elements of direction. There was also a call FROM some things. The call TO was like a spiritual push; this call FROM things was like a spiritual pull. Something, it was that call FROM the hungry, was pulling FROM them. We could feel it pulling us.

This thought of calling, TO, and FROM, reminded me of summer holidays I spent as a boy with my family. Our extended family would gather to relax and enjoy time together. Friends and/or cousins would be there, and would

The Call from the Hungry

say, "Come on. Do you want to play?" It might have been basketball, or baseball or volleyball, depending on the season, or what equipment had been toted in someone's vehicle. We were always engaged in some form of competition. Dad would be cooking something simple but tasty on the grill. Mom had prepared something to go with it that too was always tasty. Then, after we had settled into our communal and potentially memorable activities, mom would call us TO a picnic table, or some temporary table in the yard, "Come and eat. Lunch is ready." At first, we were too busy to stop. "We'll be right there, mom." The game couldn't end just yet; it wasn't over. Being the winner was too much to miss.

Though our obedience was seldom immediate, mom seldom had to make a second appeal. For then I would smell the food from the grill. At that point, it rarely mattered what was cooking. It smelled wonderful. This time it was not a spoken calling. It was a different form, and it was from that second direction. The calling was coming FROM the food. I was being called to it. It was inviting me. There was a call TO; that was mom's voice. But there was also a call FROM, and the second call was stronger. Inevitably, I was hungry, and I was being called by my own hunger. Without fail, someone would say, "That smells good. I'm hungry. Let's eat." And the game was over.

In this city, there was also a calling, and it involved hunger. But in this city, it was a bit different. It wasn't my hunger; it was their hunger that was calling me.

Yes, we were intending to focus on those who had an interest in spiritual transformation. But that was the focus TO something. Our focus was TO-wards those with an interest. Just like the food on the grill, though, there was another,

The Call from the Hungry

stronger calling. There was a call, "We're hungry", FROM the lost of the city. There was a call FROM souls, "We need to be saved". Our ears had been opened. As it was for the servant of Elisha, whose eyes were opened to see the heavenly host assembled to protect them, our ears were opened to hear a host of souls. We could hear a strong cry FROM the hungry.

This call from the hungry was compelling. It was a strong spiritual experience. The calling had not changed; it had taken on a new dimension. It came from a different direction. It overshadowed us with great, powerful motivation. Calling became stronger again and richer in purpose.

At the same time, and as it has been with so many other things, this strong, spiritual, emotional passion had to be coupled to be effective. There was, again, a practical component that was also important.

Saying, "We tried", was not enough. Our response had to be effective. To answer this resounding call required that we be effective in marketing. Ava had said, "Marketing seems like such a nasty thought, doesn't it?" My truthful response was, "Yes, it does, but we have to get the word out." When people heard the term 'marketing', they thought of sales and money, but marketing was more than that. "Yes, marketing sounds impersonal and even manipulative", I would say. "But I learned from these online materials that marketing is also about motivation. And that we do want. We want to motivate people to connect. We need to connect them to Jesus. We also need to connect them to our church."

In this new world, there was a new media for connection. To be effective, we needed to connect electronically with people (websites, social media, email,

The Call from the Hungry

etc.).

We needed to create websites. We will talk about social media soon, but we found from online materials said, "People use websites more than social media to find a church. Websites are a solid tool to reach people. They don't change constantly like social media. What they will find isn't opinions; it is official statements of a church's positions."

There were specific things that needed to be on our website(s). This time, Ava had done her online homework. "Websites are the best place to state the church's vision, its values, and ways to give. Home pages should be kept to one page, with a compelling message. The message should include information about the church, what they will experience, and how they can attend." We also learned to be careful with tricky domain names. We tried to use domain names that people could say. And many times, domain names had already been purchased with extensions like '.com', '.org', etc. So, we had to be flexible with extensions.

Certainly, we needed to use social media effectively. It was my turn to find online direction. Whereas websites were best to attract new contacts, the online experts said, "Social media is better for church members. Members can stay in contact with each other, learn of events, etc." But there were multiple social media platforms. Some were more popular in one area, while others might be more popular somewhere else. So it was up to us to choose the social media platform that was appropriate for our area.

We weren't really savvy social media experts. One of our friends who had already been through this advised, "Consider buying ads. You might also use things like ad words, and proximity filters. Post events on your social media

The Call from the Hungry

platform. And yes, you want to track the number of 'likes' you get. It's the best measure of what's working." But just having a social media page wasn't enough. We needed to update at least one social media platform per week. We hardly knew how to populate one effectively in the first place. Now we had to constantly do updates effectively as well. "Do you two think you could do that?", I asked Daniel and Mia. With big grins, they said, "Dad, it's easy. Everybody can do it. Well, except for old folks. So, I guess we can help." They couldn't contain their glee, but I hope that in there somewhere they were actually happy to contribute. I sure was happy they could do it.

We also needed to use emails effectively. Yes, email was still relevant. In fact, we 'learned' that, in many cases, email was just as effective as social media, but I doubted our children knew that yet. There were email-based marketing tools that could be used for newsletters and special announcements. And, "Thank the Lord!", at an entry level, some of them were free.

In spite of the obvious attention to electronic media, there were physical things, that still could not be overlooked. Print materials needed to be effective. Some of those materials would come directly from our website and social media. They all needed to be of good quality. We chose to use a laser printer and card stock.

Signage and banners also had to be used effectively. That too needed to be of good quality. It was important for parking and entry to the building to be easy. Ava insisted, "That's a good start. Getting inside the building is only the first step though. Communication inside the building needs to be clear as well. Our signs needed to make it easy for people

The Call from the Hungry

to find the sanctuary, classrooms, bathrooms, etc."

All of this was about being effective in answering the call from the hungry. We had gotten past the distasteful thought of marketing as evil. But marketing was more than tools. Marketing included methods. If we were going to be effective, marketing and motivation had to go beyond 'first contact'. I asked myself, "What does that term, 'first contact', mean?" It ended up being more straight-forward than I thought. Quoting from one of the church-related sources, "After their first visit, keep marketing. Follow up. Track results. Be honest about results, and make corrections."

But the challenge was worth the investment. We had a lot to learn about marketing, and how to conscientiously apply it to the church. There was really no choice. We had heard the call. This time the call wasn't just from the Lord; it was from the hungry.

Again, Daniel was quietly doing his part. He had already given us good advice on an 'elevator speech'. In that business class, they had also talked about customer focus. He even talked about our church in class. There was more sound advice, "The focus is on them, not your church. Think of them as customers. Develop a customer profile. Find out what will attract them. Ask yourself, 'How can you make it easy for them to get involved?'"

Then I was told something that stirred me. It changed how I thought about communicating. It was from a seasoned church planter who had studied human behavior in his devotion to his calling. I told him, "I am focused strongly on getting the information out." This was his response, "That's normal, but it's not enough. Information alone will not be effective. Focus on how they will respond. Absolutely, be

The Call from the Hungry

truthful, but appeal to their emotions. For response and emotion are stronger than information."

Then he finished with words that still compel me to the harvest, "Get ready. Expect hungry people. They are there. They will respond. It's their call that's driving you."

READING GUIDE POINTS:
1. The call of God is both a call TO some things and a call FROM some things
2. The call TO and the call FROM are linked in God's harmony and purpose
3. The call of the Church TO those interested in the Gospel is linked with the call FROM those that are hungry for the Gospel
4. There is a compelling call from the lost in your city
5. To reach those hungry voices that are calling, we must understand what motivates them
6. Emails, websites, social media and developing technologies are new tools to reach the hungry
7. Practical, physical things like signs and banners must be of high quality to be effective
8. Keep reaching after their first visit
9. Focus on response; emotion connects stronger than information
10. Expect hungry people

> **References from:**
> ***Effective Christianity: Managing Life's Projects***
> - Chapter 4, page 36
>   - Spiritually effective people take action
> - Chapter 4, page 38
>   - Spiritually effective people see results
> - Chapter 4, pages 38-39
>   - Spiritually effective people are fulfilled in seeing God's will accomplished
> - Chapter 5, pages 49-50
>   - Be honest when you review results
> - Chapter 5, pages 50-51
>   - Be willing to acknowledge that improvements are needed

The Cultural Leader

Yesterday there was a squabble between Daniel and Mia. What they actually said I don't remember. What it was about didn't matter. Whatever sparked the trouble, the core issues were usually feelings and fairness.

Our children were good children. We were very proud of them. Childhood was an uneasy subject among adolescents. They imagined themselves to be adults, and certainly deserved respect. Many times, each parent of an adolescent had heard, "Stop treating me like a child." They may have also heard, "I should be treated like an adult." Avoiding the argument was difficult. Truthfully, they weren't adults yet; they were adolescent children. And whatever their age, they weren't perfect. Ava felt strongly about this, "The truth is that pastor's children are just like everyone else's children. They make mistakes. They need correction. And you must love them without question no matter what happens." I agreed wholeheartedly, and felt no reason to make the point any stronger.

Knowing this, we expected trouble at times. We wished we wouldn't have to address it, but no child gave parents that luxury. More than once, I told Ava, "I no longer need to pray for patience or wisdom. I am a father. I love them, but the children push me beyond the maturity I currently possess." When they were younger, it seemed easier to calm the storm, but hormones were effective. Serenity took longer as they got older.

It was easy to get lost in the moment, but as parents we learned much from this. While they stretched us beyond our limits, our children taught us invaluable lessons. The impact would be unforgettable. They taught us of patience and unfailing love. We learned of bonds that could not be broken. There was joy for every good thing we saw them do. Faith in doing what's right was restored. We could not describe what it meant to know the love they returned to us. Nor could we express well the immeasurable satisfaction of seeing their growth. That was our reward. For them, there was the unselfish acknowledgement that honored them for what they had become, knowing that, in the end, it was up to them.

There was another lesson that our children taught us. It applied to our church. We would do our best to help people when there were disagreements. During those times when I struggled to get people to agree with each other, Ava would say, "Just as it was with our children, we can't solve every issue in the church either. They have to learn to get along with each other. Pray for them. Then we have to believe in them and the Lord."

We were determined to do our best. We needed to be examples in so many ways. None was more important than being examples to our children. And being an example started in our home.

I wanted Daniel to treat his mother with honor. The best way to do that was to show her honor myself. I did my best to demonstrate honor to my beautiful companion. But a young man's respect was more than just towards his mother. He needed to learn to treat others with respect. I insisted he also show respect to his sister. He and Mia had their disagreements. We expected that. But one thing was not allowed. Constantly, it seemed, I told him, "Even in disagreement, you will treat your sister with respect."

The Cultural Leader

Ava did her part as an example also. She was a beautiful example of showing honor to her husband. For that, I was grateful. Mia was blessed by that great example. In fairness, both Ava and I insisted she show respect for her brother. Folklore said that boys were rough and sometimes mean, and that girls were always kind and sweet. Our son, as wonderful as he was, sometimes proved the first part of that statement to be true. On the other hand, every parent of a daughter knew that imperfection was not gender-specific. Sometimes it was me, but usually it was Ava who would say to Mia, "It's not always your brother. I understand girls, more than your father. Girls can be unkind, even cruel, at times. It applies to both of you. You will treat your brother with respect too."

We determined we would do our very best to be good examples in how we treated others. That started in our home, it carried over into the church, and finally into our community as well.

As had been said before, church issues would arise occasionally. After dealing with a church skirmish, Ava shook her head in exasperation, "Edwin, isn't the Holy Ghost supposed to make us all get along, and prevent this kind of trouble?" My answer came a little later, "The truth is that's not going to happen, and it's probably better that way. Yes, the church needs to be an example of harmony, but it's still a community needing His grace. In that vein, the church needs to also be an example of forgiveness, reconciliation and listening."

Dealing with our children had already taught us that great people were still people, and they would have issues. Squabbles were unavoidable. That had been said. That

The Cultural Leader

sounded like the end of the matter. "Accept it", it was also said. But this is where church culture was important. The culture in which the squabbles arose might well determine whether squabbles were resolved or festered without end.

The culture of the church would not be an accident. Culture and behavior were inseparable. God had an expectation of our behavior. As such, He had an expectation of the culture among us. As the leader, I could have said, "I have no control of culture." But that wasn't true. Like it or not, though, I had to acknowledge, "Church leaders needed to accept this responsibility. In the home, parents set the tone, or culture, of that home. That leadership will be tested, but parents can never relinquish that responsibility. Similarly, in the church, the pastor is responsible for the culture." What a sobering acknowledgment that was.

Culture, then, was not accidental. It was intentional. Clearly, the culture of the church had to be different. New converts were coming from the culture of the world. They weren't just coming from something; they were coming to something. They were coming to the church. They needed to be transformed. This new life had to be different.

With this responsibility came challenge. A mentor had warned, "Culture will be challenged by some. It's a new discipline and a new outlook for many. Some will intentionally challenge discipline. Others may challenge a lifestyle that isn't easy or comfortable. But actually, those people are few. For many others, it's not intentional at all. The "challenge" is innocent. Their development is an unfolding process. They simply need understanding and patience." Nonetheless, culture had to be guarded, and as the pastor, I had to say, "I accept that responsibility."

The Cultural Leader

The primary elements of church culture were: the message or cultural values, the model or example set, and teaching.

The keystone of values arose yet again. The cultural message arose from the church's value statement. Those values were clearly stated. They were listed on our website:

> Focus on Jesus Christ
> Respect for others
> Service to others
> Being examples in the community
> Excellence in all we do

These values were a central element in our launch plan.

As the pastor, I had to set the example. I had accepted the responsibility, and proclaimed my calling to it. Ava and I were doing our very best to be examples. We would represent the values our church proclaimed.

It was an important part of our life as a family. I impressed on Daniel and Mia how important our church's culture was, "I can't take the issue of church culture lightly. I can't allow our church to do so either. It's not just about our family. Our church is an example of Jesus Christ in everything it does. Who we are matters." Soberingly, that example might well impact someone's eternal destiny. Earlier, I mentioned church squabbles, and whether church culture helped to see them resolved, or allowed them to fester. This was a great example of the importance of church culture. Church harmony was not the only impact of squabbles. Bitterness could arise, and put souls in peril.

The Cultural Leader

The last critical element was teaching. I made a point to emphasize, not only our values, but the importance of teaching those values. "We will teach what we value. The standard for values cannot only be by example. It has to be taught as well. Everyone who participates in our church will know our values. Everyone who accepts the responsibility of leadership will be expected to exemplify those values." I added regular teaching on this topic to our teaching plan.

READING GUIDE POINTS:
1. Learning to take responsibility for culture starts in your home
2. Your children will have disagreements; so will the members of your church
3. The pastor is responsible for the culture of the church
4. Culture must be intentional
5. It will take time for new converts to convert to the culture of the church
6. The primary elements in setting church culture are message, example and teaching

---

References from:
Effective Christianity: Managing Life's Projects
- Chapter 11, pages 156-158
    - Spiritually effective people maintain their spiritual priorities
- Chapter 11, pages 161-162
    - Effectiveness is ordained by godly principles, demonstrated by spiritual maturity and driven by divine vision

Practical Matters

Developing a Long-Term Plan

I was sitting on the floor. Pieces were scattered everywhere. Some were in bags. There was a box, now tossed across the room. On it was a picture of the beautiful, but as yet unfinished, article what was soon to be a part of our home.

Perhaps we should back up. My lovely Ava saw this tempting item that we had to have. With excitement, she said, "Edwin, I saw the picture on the box. When it's all assembled, it will look so nice. The instructions are really simple. It only takes a few simple tools. I don't know what all of them are, but I know you do. Dear, I have so much confidence in you. It will be easy." Note that she wasn't going to assemble it. No, it would be her husband, this great man that could do anything, that would surely have no trouble whatsoever doing this simple job.

Never mind this thing about being a man of God, called to great spiritual battles. That had nothing to do with this. It was more primordial that that. As her husband, and the man of the house, it was still my duty. Calling didn't excuse me from my responsibilities to my family. Right? Who else should it be? We weren't aristocrats with servants to do our menial work. We were common people devoted to a strong personal work ethic. As though she hadn't already said enough, Ava went even further, "Remember all of those times you've taught about being a spiritual leader You do want to be an example to other husbands and fathers, don't you? As I recall, being a pastor of principle, you taught that no husband, no father, no, not even the pastor, had any excuse to neglect his family. But none of that matters", she said with the smile of a

Developing a Long-Term Plan

trusting, adoring wife, "I know I can count on you."

Somewhere, probably in the strewn box, were instructions. I wasn't sure. As anxious as I was to complete my duty as quickly as possible, I forced myself to find the instructions. It contained a list of all the parts necessary to transform this mass of pieces into the wonderful keepsake we would both take great joy in knowing we had done ourselves. To be honest, I'm not sure which item I should identify with this story. If it was a song, there were many verses. It was repeated many times.

Thankfully, all of parts A and B were there. On occasion, there were even a few extra parts. Sadly, this bonus would inevitably make me question what I had missed in the transformation.

These were supposedly instructions after all. So, I began with step one, and ploddingly followed the prescribed steps.

I had to scratch my head a few times. I envisioned what the figure for some steps was showing me. More than once, while I was holding things together like I was playing Twister, I realized the part I needed could not be reached. I set things down, got the part, and contorted myself again.

Realizing I would pay for my exertion, and frustrated with all of the resets to fetch parts, I asked the obvious question. "This is taking a lot of time. Do I really need those instructions?" In my middle-aged temptation, somehow, providence guided me. I looked at the remaining parts, and recognized my ignorance. I couldn't guess where each part went, and, if it mattered, in what order.

Well, I proved that my wife's confidence was well-founded. Ava praised my prowess, "I knew you could do it.

Developing a Long-Term Plan

Edwin, you're a wonderful husband." Finally, there was a well-deserved kiss. With her help, my prowess became legend. She often presented me as the example to others faced with a similar dilemma. Most often, that praise was to the assistance of my children.

The truth was that my prowess wasn't a particular skill. It was simply learning to take the necessary steps beforehand, and following the planned activities. Order led to the desired end. Someone had taken the time to put together a plan. They determined all that was necessary, parts, steps, and order, to finish successfully. To ignore that plan would almost certainly have led to failure.

We had accepted our calling. We had responded obediently, and positioned ourselves to fulfill it. A few preliminary steps had been taken, but for the plan to unfold, there had to be a plan.

Rather than jumping frenetically into activity, we took pause, and developed a long-term plan. We wouldn't just start doing things. We didn't how many pieces there were. Did we have them all? And if we didn't know what pieces were necessary, we surely didn't know in what order to use them.

The temptation to focus on activity was strong. This planning seemed to be slowing us down. However, as it was with the do-it-yourself projects, taking the time to plan up front would help ensure we got the right things done first, and would save us time in the end.

In school, we had learned of General Eisenhower, who would then become President Eisenhower. I remembered a quote from him about planning: "Plans are nothing; planning is everything."

Developing a Long-Term Plan

We also realized that eventually, and hopefully soon, we would not be the only ones following this plan. It must have been the Lord. Somehow, He helped us to know these new people would also need that plan. Followers probably wouldn't be able to follow our dream. How could they? That vision was in our mind. As such, it was not concrete. The level of detail they required was missing. On the other hand, they could follow our plan. If we took our vision, transforming it and documenting it as a long-term plan, others could follow it.

If others were to follow, as a starting point, we needed to define the strategic goals for the church. What kind of church would we be? How would the church be governed? These may have seemed obvious or intuitive. We should simply follow the Bible, some would have said. But there were specifics that needed to be clarified. For example, what role would the church play in this community? We had to start somewhere. Knowing that, what demographic group would be the initial focus? What external ministries and community programs would the church support?

Some administrative issues needed to be clarified as well. One pressing question was how soon the church would be financially independent. Some clarity was needed to explain how the church would manage its operations. Income, giving and staff expenses were primary examples. This would become a key determinant in how we would use checking and savings accounts, and what financial software would be appropriate. It would also guide us in how we would seek professional guidance externally.

The long-term plan would identify key milestones and high-level activities. There were many. These were a few of

Developing a Long-Term Plan

them: projected launch date, decision on our initial location, what the key leadership positions and decisions would be, what major purchases were expected, if and what kind of loans would be needed and projected dates for application, when teams would be formed, when Sunday School would begin, what financial management tools would be needed, when a church board would be established, when legal documents for incorporation and bylaws would be incorporated.

We also included some important family matters in the plan. Ava was a bit concerned, "How much of that are you going to share?" "I don't know", I said, "but they're very important to us." Where we would live would be important, of course. But just as important, we needed to establish what home meant. Some rules and guidelines needed to be established. We addressed how the children might be involved in school, and how active we should be with them. Then was the matter of vacations and family activities. Ava was firm about this, "Dear, there has to be a commitment from the beginning about our family, or there will always be reasons to neglect our time together." We had to commit to and project how soon we would transition in our jobs. This meant balancing our calling and our financial responsibility to ourselves.

In all of that, it was important that we listen and pay attention to our family. Daniel and Mia were important. This would be a great sacrifice for them, and they needed to be heard. As parents, and as husband and wife, we could not neglect each other. As Ava had already said, I repeated to the children, "We are a family, and our priority as a family has to be firm."

Developing a Long-Term Plan

    This would be the first of many plans. We were starting to realize that practical matters were more important to our calling than we had realized before. We did not regret having a long-term plan. It served us well and often. It became the basis for so many other steps and decisions. It was documented, but not set in stone. There would be changes, but we had a starting point. It took considerable effort. Some things took time and prayer to decide. We really weren't well-versed in managing resources and schedules, and things like that. But those things would certainly follow.

    When it was complete, there was some satisfaction, and a sense of peace. We knew we had taken a great, early step in assuring fulfillment. More than ever, we knew the things we were to do. It was documented in goals and activities. There were specifics we did not have before. And with those specifics, we would be able to connect with others in this great vision.

Developing a Long-Term Plan

READING GUIDE POINTS:
1. Failing to plan leads to failure
2. Resist the temptation to get started without first planning
3. The first and most important plan is the long-term plan
4. The long-term plan identifies the strategic goals of the church
5. Effective administration is critical to the success of a church
6. Define key administrative matters like finances, governance and church operations in the strategic plan
7. Include your family early in your planning
8. Having good plans gives a sense of confidence and peace

Developing a Long-Term Plan

> **References from:**
> ***Effective Christianity: Managing Life's Projects***
> - Chapter 4, page 36
>   - Effective people see their actions not as pursuing their will, but as a response to His will
>   - Effective people accept that they will make mistakes, but move forward anyway
> - Chapter 4, page 37
>   - Fulfilling God's will is about the balance between submission and responsibility
> - Chapter 4, page 38
>   - A good plan expects problems and prepares for them
> - Chapter 4, page 43
>   - By responding to dreams with action, spiritually effective people know the joy of dreams fulfilled
> - Chapter 6, page 52
>   - The principles of project management are legitimate for the Church
>   - There is a legitimate method for spiritually effective people to practice project management

Developing a Long-Term Plan

> **References from:**
> ***Effective Christianity: Managing Life's Projects***
> - Chapter 6, page 56
>   - Listening is more than the hearing of words. True listening is accompanied by following.
>   - Talking is more than reciting or saying of words. It is accompanied by trust.
> - Chapter 6, page 58
>   - The most vibrant spiritual person will only be fulfilled if they know they have been effective
>   - Effective listening is coupled with response
> - Chapter 6, page 59
>   - An effective life demands action
> - Chapter 6, page 60
>   - Passive faith is a contradiction
> - Chapter 6, page 61
>   - Most project failures can be traced to the failure to capture and maintain requirements. The cause for this failure is assumption.
> - Chapter 6, page 65
>   - Planning can be exciting, for planning is coupled with visions and dreams
> - Chapter 6, page 67
>   - Prepare for success

Developing a First-Year Plan

The Lord's resources weren't limited. As He had done throughout the Bible, He showed He could use people outside of the church for His purpose. The most well-known story was Balaam. Even animals were used for His purpose. So many times, in the prophets, the Lord said He would use ungodly rulers to serve His purpose in correcting sin in His chosen people.

I was in a business one day. The business was established and doing well. I could see that steps had been taken to keep current. Displays were new. New items were in prominent places. I had a rare opportunity to have a conversation with the owner. Normally, there would be plenty of people needing attention. The Lord provided opportunity for me, and was about to speak through this unsaved messenger.

We had been in the store before. We had done our best to make connections with others. The owner knew who we were and why we were in the city. He asked, "How is the church doing?" I told Him, "Things are developing. We believe the Lord will help us succeed." He said, "Pastor, I appreciate what you're doing. You're doing a good thing. We need good churches." Continuing, he said, "As a business man, I know it isn't easy to get something started. Success isn't an accident. You can't just wait for it to happen. It's not just about 'what', but 'when' matters too." With probing sincerity, he challenged me, "If you don't mind me asking, where do you want to be one year from now?"

I guess I wasn't prepared for that simple inquiry. My 'elevator speech' didn't seem to be the answer. As quickly as I

Developing a First-Year Plan

could think, I mentioned some things I wanted to happen. The things I was currently focused on came to mind more easily. In my attempt to answer, though, I realized that I hadn't yet made 'when' specific. It was a bit of a surprise, but another lesson was learned. One of the hardest things to do was to clearly state what I wanted. Now I needed to answer not only what I wanted, but when as well. The challenge was compounded, but the challenge was on.

Decisions had to be made. Priorities had to be set. While explaining the conversation with the store owner, I asked myself, "What should be accomplished in the next year? What would not? Without setting priorities, I may constantly be distracted by things that aren't needed until a later date. I needed focus to prevent distraction." As the business owner had said, "Success isn't an accident."

I had to write it down. Documenting my priorities was important for me. It was even more important for others. I asked Ava, "Who else needs to know? Do you think this dream is known to everyone, or only to me?" Her response, "If it's a dream, then probably only you really know it." Another realization dawned on me. Dreams and plans were not the same. It was nearly impossible to follow someone else's dream, but you could follow their plan. Dreams were clouded in the heart. My dream was clouded in my heart. My plan would be clear, so that all could follow.

I had a long-term plan. I started there. However, those things were mostly strategic. There wasn't a particular timeline. They were aspirational goals I wanted to ultimately achieve. Now I had to translate some of those goals into things I needed to accomplish in the next year. It was time to define some operational goals.

Developing a First-Year Plan

I had accepted, with the long-term plan, that planning was part of being spiritual. Moreso than with the aspirational goals in the long-term plan, I knew I could fall into the trap of believing I was taking God's will into my own hands. Now I was getting very specific. The question still loomed, "Whose plan would this be?" Was I still following God's plan? I risked making it my own. Sensitivity was my continuing responsibility, but it was still my responsibility to take action in accordance with God's direction.

Again, I had to resist the excuses:

"I don't have time to plan".

"Planning takes too much time".

If I was going to succeed, I had to force myself to push. I told the Lord with earnestness, "Excuses will only hold me back from seeing your will fulfilled. Purpose drives me beyond excuses."

Gideon was a great example to me of planning and sensitivity. He seemed an unlikely hero. Many sermons had been preached proclaiming God's determination overcoming Gideon's tepidness and fear. Gideon certainly was unqualified. He, like Moses, was fearful. But he responded when God spoke. He asked questions, but he also took action.

God re-directed Gideon many times. Gideon had a plan, but it wasn't exactly how God wanted to do things. But God never rebuked Gideon for responding. As Gideon kept responding, God led him one step at a time. God narrowed the number substantially, but there was a point often overlooked. How did those 32,000 men get there? They were there because Gideon took action. Then Gideon let God change his direction.

I took steps and came up with a plan. I thought it might

Developing a First-Year Plan

change, but I had a plan. Starting with the long-term plan, I developed a project plan for the next year.

Truthfully, 'I' was 'we'. Together, Ava and I determined which of the items in the long-term plan needed to be accomplished in the next year. We put them in an order that seemed most logical at the time. We then assigned dates or milestones for each of those items. We did our best to define what actions would be needed to accomplish each of those items and how long each of those actions would take.

That was difficult enough, but the next steps were a bit harder. We had to decide who would have responsibility for each item as a whole, and for each specific action, who would be the person doing that action. In theory, that sounded simple enough. Reality was more difficult. In some cases, I looked at Ava, and said, "This responsibility belongs to a resource we don't yet have." A cost was then assigned for each action. We did our best to put the tasks into a schedule. Lastly, we translated all of those costs into a budget.

As with the long-term plan, when finally complete, we were happy. In thanking Ava, I said, "I'm happy with the result, and all you contributed to it. I don't consider us to be project managers, but this felt like what a good project manager would do. Ava said, "I'm happy too. That exercise was challenging, but we now have a plan."

The next question was whether the plan was realistic. Assessing that would take some help. We could do our best to be objective, but we felt it better to get someone else to look at the plan. We still had some mentors that were good as "sounding boards." We asked them to tell us if this plan was realistic. If they were to challenge some things, that was acceptable. We wanted to find someone else we could trust

Developing a First-Year Plan

to be objective about our results.

With this detailed action plan that had been reviewed by mentors, we began taking action. At times, we felt like Gideon. We had to adapt. Some things were late. Some things costed more than planned. Adjustments were necessary. But we had a good starting point, and a basis for adapting.

This was crucial in our success. We couldn't give up, and with a solid plan, we were never tempted to do so. To any who questioned the value of planning, our experience proved differently. We would say to them, "You may have to change the plan, but without a plan, you have no hope of success."

READING GUIDE POINTS:
1. 'When" has to be set
2. Others can follow your plans; they can't follow your dreams
3. Start by translating your long-term goals into plans for the first year
4. Effective planning requires spiritual sensitivity and responsive action
5. For each item in the plan, identify specific actions, key resources and costs
6. Have others review your plans
7. Having a plan gives you the ability to adapt rather than give up

Developing a First-Year Plan

> **References from:**
> ***Effective Christianity: Managing Life's Projects***
> - Chapter 1, page 3
>   - Planning, organization and strategy are of great spiritual benefit. Theys help us to be more effective.
>   - People may be fascinated by your dreams, but they have confidence in your plans
> - Chapter 2, page 11
>   - Being practical requires setting goals, organization, planning, and managing to a purpose. There must be focus on achieving specific objectives. The end result is a more effective, more creative, and more productive life.
> - Chapter 2, page 13
>   - It is a wonderful step to commit to a goal God has shown you. Spiritual maturity means taking the right steps to get there.

Developing a First-Year Plan

References from:
Effective Christianity: Managing Life's Projects

- Chapter 6, page 60
  - A project is a collection of activities to accomplish a specific goal
- Chapter 6, page 64
  - Every project has goals, costs and risks. Commitment is required.
- Chapter 6, page 65
  - The Lord may change the plan. Some then say there is no need for planning, but planning gets you to the place where He can show you the new plan.
- Chapter 7, page 69
  - If we lose control, we may get ahead of God's plan, or distract ourselves with things that are not central to our calling. We are then headed on the path of failure.
- Chapter 7, page 70
  - For our visions to be realized, it is critical that they be clearly defined.
- Chapter 8, page 81
  - Flexibility requires obedience, focus and diligence
- Chapter 10, page 90
  - Understanding there is risk increases our likelihood of surviving battles of faith
- Chapter 10, page 95
  - Too often we assume things that we should not. We should not assume that:
    - Everything will always go well
      - Everyone will support you
      - You know how to plan your own future

Building Teams

On this journey to plant a church, I was drawn again to the story of the Apostles. The title itself drew me. It was called the Book of Acts after all. As such, it focused on the ACTIONS of the Apostles. The authorship attracted my attention as well. It was written by a historian who chronicled the history of the Apostolic era. This book focused on more than actions though.

With great consonance in my spirit and my desire to be effective in His calling, I felt the Lord tell me, "This was also a great story of team-building." Looking at this great story again, I saw it. It was more than a story of Peter and Paul, or Timothy and Silas. It was more than missionary exploits and churches in places I had never been. As important as it was, it was more than a revelation of the plan of salvation. Yes, it was all of those things. The Lord opened my eyes to so much more.

It felt like He gave me a long list of things to notice. A few of them I had seen, but not in this current relevance. To my heart, He and His Word were saying to me:

"Look at the number of characters in this story."

"Look at the great diversity of their personalities, skills, gifts and talents."

"Take note of the great accomplishments of this team, considering the great differences in personalities."

"Appreciate the leading of the Holy Spirit to guide the Apostles in initiating great leaders like Paul and Barnabas."

"Appreciate the leadership of Paul in establishing new works and appointing effective successors."

"Appreciate the role of Barnabas in supporting Paul, standing for his own direction, and believing in John Mark."

"Appreciate how Timothy and Titus stepped up to leadership roles, and responded to mentoring."

Building Teams

"Appreciate so many little-known characters whose leadership is largely unheralded."

The Lord challenged me. Like so many others, I had preached about the days of the Apostles. I had exhorted to achieve that level of effectiveness while lamenting our failure. This challenge was not a general command, "Be like the Apostles." No, it was more specific and actionable than that. He challenged me to build teams as the Apostles did. To accept that challenge, I needed that repeating blend of things spiritual and practical. I needed to wisely blend the leading of the Holy Ghost with the skills of resource management and scheduling.

With nearly every part of this, Ava and I worked on it together. There was a long-term plan and a first-year plan already. The details of the first-year plan had become an urgent focus. In that plan were the launch team, the core team and volunteer staff. Establishing those teams demanded yet another level of detail if the plan was to be managed effectively. There needed to be a separate, clear plan for each team, and a separate profile for each.

Since it was needed first, Ava and I began working on the Launch Team. Once again, her balance was critical to our success. We started to outline characteristics of the team. It would be temporary and outreach-oriented. But when we got to determining who could be on the team, we hit a snag.

Saying what seemed obvious, "If they're going to represent the church, they must be saved. They needed to be baptized in the name of Jesus and filled with the Holy Spirit." I was ready to move on to other decisions about the team. Remember the point about practical things. Sometimes, it was just having or getting a practical perspective. That's where Ava made a difference. She was thinking ahead.

"Who's going to be on the Core Team. Is it the same people as those on the Launch Team? If it is, why do we need two teams with the same people? If not, and everybody must be saved, will we have enough people? Salvation is important for sure. But we

Building Teams

may have to be practical. We're here because there's no Apostolic church in this city. We're not overflowing with saved people yet."

Recognizing this reality, we paused. "You're right. It makes more sense for us to decide who will be on the Core Team, and then finish the plans for the Launch Team. It isn't chronologically correct, but logically it's the right thing to do." As I look back, there are more occasions that I can recall where I was glad I had listened to Ava. My experience taught me that everyone called of God, no matter how anointed they are, needed someone in their life to give them another perspective.

The Core Team might be different than the Launch Team, and its membership might be different as well. Whereas the Launch Team would be temporary and outreach oriented, the Core Team would be long-term and discipleship-oriented. There was one very important distinction from the Launch Team membership.

With some conviction, I told Ava, "The Core Team should only be open to strong members, people who are saved. That might limit the size of the team significantly at first. If that's the case, then so be it. These will become the key leaders, the spiritual 'backbone', that will sustain the church beyond launch." There was no hesitation in Ava's response, "Yes, I agree. We may have to flex a bit with the Launch Team, but the Core Team is different".

The Launch Team was linked to one event, launch. There would be no singular event or goal for the Core Team. Their goal was much broader, to sustain a strong church.

Returning to the Launch Team, it needed energetic people who were active and supportive. It seemed odd at first, but reality compelled me, "It may not be required that all of the Launch Team be saved, or at least not yet. It will be open to anyone who is willing to help launch the church."

The Launch Team would be evangelistic in their orientation, but then there was another unexpected recognition, "They don't all have to be evangelists. They need to all work together as an effective evangelistic team though." I was convinced that people

Building Teams

with administrative strength could be important members of an evangelistic team. If all were working together to support evangelism and make the team effective, then each member who contributed to that end would be important. It required that each team member value the other members of the team. That requirement would be reinforced, and the same principle would be applied to every team.

The last step was to establish goals for the Launch Team. Those goals included the following:

> Launch date
> Number of people contacted
> Number of contacts recorded
> Number of people attending church services

The last team wasn't actually a team. It was the volunteer staff. In time, there would be paid positions on the staff. But for the foreseeable future, there was no choice but to rely on volunteers. Volunteer staff would be people holding administrative and ministerial leadership roles. They would help on a personal level in ministering to new members, people in struggle or crisis, and with contacts that were not part of the church. In addition to serving the needs of the members, these volunteers played another important role. They would help the church to be credible in a business sense. It seemed like a lot of responsibility. "Where else can we go to find these people?", I asked Ava. This time she paused for a few thoughtful seconds, then said, "I don't think we have any 'other' people; they will have to come from the Core Team." So, with continuing realism in managing resources, it was decided that it was best if the volunteer staff, at the start, was a subset of the Core Team.

Thinking ahead was not over. There had to be clarity about the future of these roles. With that caution in mind, I said, "We need to make it clear, at the very beginning, whether any of these positions is considered to be temporary or permanent. Even as

Building Teams

volunteers, we should be clear that there is no promise or obligation. Some of these positions may only be needed for a short while. And whoever helps as a volunteer may not be the same person if that position or role becomes permanent." Ava concurred, "We must be wary of promising permanent positions too early. Some of these volunteers may not even be permanent members of the church. If they have been 'loaned' by another church, the duration of their service should be as clear as possible."

Managing these volunteers appeared to be the most challenging responsibility as resource managers. Truthfully, all of it would be challenging. There would likely be unsaved people on the Launch Team. The size of the Core Team might be limited for some time. I had to be thankful and careful in utilizing, respecting and controlling expectations of volunteers. In all of it, I could not forget that part of my responsibility would be to see spiritual development and fulfillment among all team members and staff.

Building teams would be rewarding and challenging. It forced upon me a question, "We have defined the role of these teams, but what is my role?" "There will be more people involved now. Personalities, teamwork, conflict, coordination are all part of it. How do I prepare myself?" As I prayed about this developing need, some things came to mind. I believed it was from the Lord.

First and foremost, I needed to have the leading of the Lord and to be prayerful. I acknowledged His leading in prayer, "Lord, this is not my church, these are not my teams, and these are not my resources. It is your church; these are your teams; these are divine resources devoted to your purpose. I will not take over; you must lead or I will fail." I did my best to always keep that mind.

I needed to be positive. Being positive was about more than what these teams would accomplish. I needed to be positive about the people on the teams. In prayer, I also acknowledged, "God, you have led each of these people to us; you have given them gifts and deficiencies. What you have provided will be sufficient. We are 'fitly framed'. I will trust in your calling in their lives. I will trust that

Building Teams

each of them will do their best." The best strategy would be centered around recognizing them.

I needed to be energetic, but genuine. This would not be a false energy built on continuous heightened emotion. That expectation would have been dishonest. I couldn't do it. I didn't expect it from the team. What I would model, as best I could, was a sustained endurance. We were not in a sprint, though the pace we were in at that moment felt like it. There would be struggle no doubt, but not resignation. He would give us energy to endure through struggle. That determined energy had to start with me.

I needed to be helpful. There were more important things than proving my authority. Authority was important of course. But I was called first to be their minister. Some of them may have been overlooked in the past. Some may have made mistakes in the past, and need someone to give them another chance. We were all taking a fresh start. I would believe in them. I would challenge them positively. I wouldn't withhold my thanks, demanding more than they thought they could do. I would be thankful for any and every positive contribution they made.

I would take practical steps to prepare and sustain. The first was to identify potential resources. It sounded more sterile than organic. Trying to be rational, I said to Ava, "We need to be as effective as we can with the resources He has given. The logical place to start is with the people I know: my family, and the friends that I know." Ava replied, "Of course. That makes sense. We have to start somewhere. But there will be others. We have capable people. God will provide more capable people. He will use those capabilities. They will rise to the challenge." I completed the list with as many names as I knew. When the exercise was done, there was also a list of resources needed.

I began to cross-reference this list of resources, many of them unnamed, with a chart. The chart was divided into sections for each team. For each team, the mission was identified. What was the purpose? Why did this team exist? The number of

Building Teams

positions or slots needed for each team was also identified. As much as possible, a job description was created for each position or role. This was especially important for volunteer staff.

Staffing all of these teams required ongoing attention. Goals were established for filling each roster. There would be additions, and yes subtractions, so it was necessary to keep the rosters current. Just like managing a schedule, progress was tracked. As necessary, the plan was adapted and adjustments were made. Administration was important.

READING GUIDE POINTS:
1. The Book of Acts demonstrates one of the best examples of team building
2. Each team you build needs a separate, clear plan and a distinct profile
3. Until you have an established, larger church, you may need to be flexible in who you can allow on your teams
4. The Launch Team will be temporary and outreach oriented
5. The Core Team will be long-term and discipleship-oriented
6. At first, your staff will likely be a volunteer team
7. Create a staffing plan that clearly identifies who will be on what team
8. As the leader, it is your responsibility to be led of the Lord, and to be positive, energetic and helpful
9. As the leader, it is your responsibility to ensure their roles help in their spiritual development
10. You must trust that the Lord is providing the resources your teams need

Building Teams

> **References from:**
> ***Effective Christianity: Managing Life's Projects***
> - Chapter 9, page 84
>   - You may need people, materials, and money. Knowing there will be challenges, join in the battle, and watch Him provide.
>   - As spiritual people, we believe:
>   - I can get the resources needed
>   - God will provide what I cannot
> - Case study, The Apostles, page 117
>   - The Apostolic team was diverse, coordinated and effective. There was no sense of superiority.
>   - They recognized and embraced their differences in leadership roles and style.
>   - This team was flexible, committed to each other, and focused ultimately on their purpose. They remained committed to each other and their common purpose through great trial and adversity.
>   - The focus was on purpose over position.
>   - These tremendous accomplishments could not have been possible without a strong, effective team. Every good leader also knows that every team member is important to that success.

The Cement of Administration

Ava and I had done our best to balance things that were clearly spiritual with more practical responsibilities. There was one very important practical matter that hadn't been addressed yet. As it turned out, pursuing it proved to be both an interesting and paradoxical discovery. It started with another conversation, and quickly reinforced just how important these practical matters were.

"OK, I'm all for doing this practical stuff. Long-term plans, first-year plans, plans to build teams, those are all important. But if we're going to be practical, shouldn't we start thinking about a location for our church, or at least for the location to launch? Are we far enough along to start on that?", I pleaded to Ava. With a shared, earnest tone, she replied, "It seems like there's so much to do before getting to the main thing. I'm not sure if it's time to make any commitments, but why can't we start looking, and get some ideas? Do you have any place in mind?" I told her, "There's a vacant building I saw that could work, I think." She gave me the reinforcement I was seeking, "Sure. Go take a look. Let's see where it leads."

After driving for a short while, I found the vacant building. It was in a nice location, in a good neighborhood. There were businesses nearby. I went in to one.

Introducing myself, I said, "I'm looking for a property for a new church. I noticed that vacant building. Do you know anything about what happened?"

Their response was very nice, "Having another church sounds like a good thing for this community. It's a good location. We aren't exactly sure what happened. A new

The Cement of Administration

business moved in about a year ago. It seemed like they were doing well. They must have been growing. A number of things were expanding. Having another successful business increased customer traffic. We were happy to see it."

"After a few months, though, it looked like the service started to decline. It was a big shame. Customers came into our store and complained about it. The business started to cut back on their hours and services provided. It wasn't looking good. Sure enough, soon there was a sign posted on the door that they had closed."

As disappointing as that was for that failed business, it looked like an opportunity for us. As Ava said, "Let's see where this leads."

There was a sign in the window identifying who the owner was, and how to contact them. I contacted the number posted on the building. The owner was helpful. I asked him what happened with the previous business. He said, "The guy had a good idea and a vision for the business. He had good ideas. The problem wasn't the product or even income. The problem was he didn't control his expenses. He was growing, and wanted to expand with that growth. But he went too fast. His expansion put him in more debt than he could manage. He didn't have a good plan for cash flow. He was counting on growth being enough, but it wasn't. He couldn't pay all of his bills and had to start cutting back. From that point, it became a downward financial spiral."

Then he made an important statement that I wouldn't forget, "A dream doesn't sustain itself. Effective planning and administration sustain a dream."

As it turned out, and as anxious as we were, it wasn't time yet for a building. As Ava had also suggested, "I'm not

The Cement of Administration

sure if it's time to make any commitments." But it was a good thing that we tried. We learned another important practical lesson.

It was a sobering lesson that applied to churches as well. Churches had to manage finances to survive and especially to grow. Once again, I bounced this realization off of my 'sounding board', Ava. "What makes this sobering", I said, "is that, if we're not careful, this church could fail. It's not like it used to be. Many church doors are closed. It's a little scary. Churches must be compliant with legal and safety issues, and so many other business issues. We're not immune. It's just like a private business."

I continued, "Besides, if we force this too soon, we'll get ahead of God's timing. I want to move forward. We need a building sometime. It feels like it should be soon. But in talking with this property owner, I knew it wasn't time yet. I'm doing my best to be responsible and patient at the same time. Stepping out of the will of God would be a disaster. In my heart, I know that. But waiting is getting so hard."

"I hear you, dear", began Ava's response. "In my prayers, I keep asking the Lord, 'Are we doing enough?' But we have to be patient. I know how hard that is for you. You want to get things done. But as my mom used to say, 'God's timing is perfect.' I believe in you, and I pray for you every day that the Lord will lead you."

Then she added, "My prayer list keeps growing. I'm praying for people we've met that need to be saved. I'm praying for a lot of 'spiritual' things. I have to add these business things to the list."

"Effective planning and administration sustain a dream", echoed in my mind. He was absolutely right. We

The Cement of Administration

didn't have the luxury of separating the administrative responsibilities from our spiritual dream. They were inseparable. Administrations was a key element in the cement that would hold our church together. To survive, our church needed good planning. Our church also had to take administrative matters seriously, or just like that failed business, the church could end up struggling.

Ava and I talked about how to handle all of these administrative responsibilities. As with nearly everything else, it was a team effort. There never came a time when I ceased relying on my wife's help. Together we prayed, and came up with yet another list of things to help us manage better:

- Both of us would talk to our mentors.
- Ava would search and come up with a list of lessons we could study online.
- She would also find a few reference books we would purchase
- I would look for software that was already available that could make things easier
- We saw that there was too much to do by ourselves. It became obvious that we needed to start identifying and talking to key people for our Core Team right away.
- I would see if there were people on the emerging Core Team that were able to help. We didn't want to distract the Launch Team from their single focus of launching, but, if necessary, we might even talk to one or two from that team as well.

This administrative reality forced more flexibility with limited team resources than I had hoped. It also forced me to deal with that reality sooner than I wanted. It would have

The Cement of Administration

been a lot easier to put this off for a while. But by waiting, it might be too late to fix things later. Remembering that failed business, I could not knowingly allow the unbearable strain it would cause by waiting. I needed to start right away on the cement that would hold things together, and get all of the help I could as soon as possible.

Ava wasted no time in completing her first assignment. "I found some things online about financial management that look like they might be good", she said. 'As soon as possible' came quickly. "Thank you dear. I knew I could count on you to keep me on track. I'll look at them right away", was my grateful response.

The next day, I did look at the online materials. It was another opportunity to take a step back, and keep my composure. These were the topics they talked about:

- Managing finances
- Financial sustainment
- Categorizing income and expenses
- Detailing a budget
- Doing financial analysis (measurements of some kind)
- Setting financial targets
- Discretionary margins
- Determined (intentional) savings

As if that wasn't enough, there was more material telling me I needed to do all of these things:

- Teach about giving and finances
- Ensure credibility and success
- Identify systems and processes
- Identify sources and accounts
- Use checking accounts only for operations

The Cement of Administration

    Use savings account (s) for special projects
    Ensure compliance with safety regulations
    The church needed by-laws and legal documents
    The church would have to be registered with the state Secretary of State

For financial management alone, one document said we should do all of these things as well:

    Use good financial software
    Create credible, clear financial reports
    Create a process for contribution statements
    Blend all of the financial reports using an 'all-in-one'
    Blend financial management and reporting with other financial activities

    It was time to find that help Ava and I had talked about. I wasn't sure what some of these things were, like discretionary margins and financial analysis, and I didn't really know how I was supposed to categorize income and expenses. I told Ava, "It's good we started now on this administrative stuff. I would hate to be down the road a lot further, and only beginning to look for the help we need."

    One of the things I learned was that a church needed people who were competent in all of these administrative skills. This thought of administrative cement wasn't just about responsibilities and requirements. It applied to resources within the church. It was another example of the church being fitly framed.

    Finding people with administrative skill proved to be more difficult than I thought. When it came to choosing a worship leader or a Sunday School teacher, there were at least a few options. There weren't many choices for things

The Cement of Administration

like financial management. There was one person among the prospective members of the Core Team that had some business financial background. He said, "I'm not the expert, but I can take the lead in talking with an accountant about financial things." For the legal documents, I contacted some pastors who let our church use their documents as guidelines. A final review by an attorney was still needed to make sure the documents were credible.

The whole purpose of these administrative things was to ensure that the right things were accomplished. Results mattered. Goals needed to be met for contacting new people and getting them to church. It was up to the Lord to save them, but if we did our part, we were confident that would happen. We set goals for baptisms and those receiving the Holy Spirit. But there were financial goals, dates for bylaws, etc. We needed to review results and make sure things were progressing in many areas.

The church had a long-term plan. On a regular basis, we would review what strategic goals had been met, and if the plan needed to be updated. Goals had been set for the Launch Team. This was a near-term plan. Were we meeting those goals? Corrections had been made for many things. We documented the leadership lessons we had learned.

Those online materials that had startled me said, "Giving and stewardship must be taught." Those items were added to the teaching plan. Our church was made possible by the giving of others. We needed to be a giving church as well. We established multiple methods for giving. Giving this much attention to money was a bit difficult. But the online materials also made an important point about fundraising:

The Cement of Administration

"Fundraising is about the mission". I needed to remember that, and teach it to our church.

One of the critical lessons learned was about this cement of administration. The lesson was that effective administration is critical for the sustainment and credibility of the church. A church must be credible in its message, and its practice. It did matter what we believed and how we lived. Those things were non-negotiable requirements to be credible in our community. But it was also essential that we have credibility with banks and creditors, and government. Administration was the cement that provided that credibility.

There was another important lesson learned from the materials we reviewed. It was about taking personal responsibility for results: "Programs don't manage; you do."

READING GUIDE POINTS:
1. Effective planning and administration sustain dreams
2. Churches must manage finances to survive and especially to grow
3. Churches must be compliant with legal, safety, and many other business issues
4. As determined as you are to see results, getting ahead of God's timing is disastrous
5. Administration is a key element in the cement that holds your church together
6. A successful church needs people who are competent in administrative skills
7. Finding key people with administrative skill may be difficult
8. Include administrative goals (financial, legal, etc.) in your plans

> **References from:**
> ***Effective Christianity: Managing Life's Projects***
> - Chapter 2, page 12
>   - All of these things seem to be in the way of what we're called to do, our spiritual focus
> - Chapter 2, page 13
>   - Being effective spiritually has a practical component
>   - It's not an either/or solution; it's an AND solution
>   - Failure because we ignore practical, administrative matters is not acceptable. People's souls are at stake. If that's true, then we need to walk this "tight rope" between spirituality and practicality
> - Chapter 2, page 16
>   - Our calling does not allow us to avoid the risk; we must somehow learn and listen to manage the two
> - Chapter 5, page 44-45
>   - Goals, planning and clear communication are critical to success
> - Chapter 5, page 45
>   - We must be clear about our goals and plans

The Cement of Administration

> **References from:**
> ***Effective Christianity: Managing Life's Projects***
> - Chapter 5, page 49
>   - We must be objective in our review
> - Chapter 6, page 52
>   - The principles of project management are legitimate for the Church. More than that, the inherent transparency, mission focus, stewardship, and effectiveness are needed.
> - Chapter 6, page 60
>   - To accomplish His will, we must set goals. They are achieved through projects.
> - Case study, Joseph, page 115
>   - Important elements in the success of Joseph and Pharaoh were strong strategic and administrative skills
> - Case study, Nehemiah, page 115
>   - The success of Nehemiah was a great example of resource management, time management and risk management
> - Case study, Fundraiser, page 115
>   - The building program fundraising campaign showed the importance of communicate problems transparently

Panic

I remember telling Ava, "Last Sunday night was a turning point. After service, I felt terrible." "Were you sick?", she asked. I replied, "No, not really. I wasn't physically sick, but I was sick in my soul."

The problem had been building all week. I had rehearsed the story in my mind so many times. For whom, I wasn't sure. Maybe I was storing it up for the Lord, as if He wasn't already aware of these thoughts, "I am just so busy. There are so many things that I have to do. I have all of these church activities, and making sure and taking time for connections. Everything needs a plan. The list of things to do just seems to never end."

Then I started talking to myself, "Yeah, I know. Don't be the lone wolf. But even with help, it seems the list of duties is unending. I'm looking, and there isn't enough of 'me', and there isn't enough of 'them'. Maybe later, but not yet."

Then there was the internal argument about priorities and commitment, "My children still need a father. My time with my wife is important. I just don't have time to prepare."

Then it happened. Panic hit. It came on fast, and it came on strong. I sat down Saturday night and asked the Lord, "Will you give me something to say for Sunday morning?" I honestly didn't know what to teach for Sunday School, the next morning. All week long, the discomfort was there, but I hadn't had the time to take care of it. Here it was the night before, and my plea continued, "Lord, I still don't have anything to say."

Now it was time for that rehearsed message to the

Panic

Lord, "Lord, I've been very busy, and I need your help." I got a little louder, and with even more fervor said, "I really need your help." Surely my earnestness and anxiety meant something in His sight. After all, everything we were doing was to plant a church in this city. I told the Lord, "We're not being lazy. My assurance is in you. You have to answer. I've done all that I can. I just need to trust you. Right? RIGHT?!"

The Lord was silent. I had no choice. Then, --- , no, I didn't! YES, I DID! I think I scolded the Lord, "I'm doing your work. HOW CAN YOU NOT ANSWER?" I didn't feel Him inspiring me with a topic or message. There was no voice from heaven. There I was, not knowing what to do, and there was nothing. I couldn't obey unless He spoke. If there was supposed to be a message in silence, it wouldn't help me tomorrow. What was I going to do?

I did something. I pulled out some old lessons and picked something I had used before. I went through my notes and made a few changes so it would be for that service. I prayed. Yes, I prayed. "Lord, I hope you'll anoint me tomorrow. I don't feel any anointing now." After that very busy week, I got to bed late, and I did not sleep well.

The next morning, I did my dutiful best. I tried to make the lesson exciting, getting louder and adding appropriate emphasis. Getting the audience to respond was always helpful. My conscience said, "Good semantics, but you know what you did."

When I was done, those wonderful people responded with support and great kindness. They told me, "You did a great job, pastor." We really had some wonderful people. They were so sincere. They wanted to do anything they could to help.

Panic

I appreciated their kindness, but I knew better. They would never suggest it, but they didn't have to. I didn't need anybody else to tell me. My heart said, "That was terrible." All night before, the Lord was silent. Now I felt the Lord was speaking. There were still no words, but now His silence seemed to speak. My attitude had been tested. I'm not sure I passed that test. "Lord, where were You when I asked for guidance?"

Then it was like a bolt of lightning hit me. I remembered what my old pastor used to say, "Some preachers are like Samson. They assume there will be anointing anytime they need it. Your calling alone doesn't assure you're always anointed. Anointing isn't automatic. It doesn't come by accident, and it shouldn't be taken for granted."

These words rolled in my mind over and over again. Then there was one last memory from my old paster, "Anointed delivery is the result of anointed preparation."

Now I heard it, "Yes, you were busy, but you weren't prepared." There couldn't be any anointing in my preparation if there was no preparation. I was reminded of someone else who was too busy. I was reminded of Moses, and the advice from his father-in-law. Moses exhausted himself every day, listening to each matter that had to be judged. He was sincerely doing his best, but he wasn't being effective. He rightly said, "I don't have enough time." I was saying the same thing. Moses could rightly say, "The responsibility for the leadership of everything is mine." I was saying the same thing. He had to change his approach. So did I.

The problem wasn't my teaching. The problem was there was no plan for my teaching. I confessed to Ava, "I've

Panic

been trying to pull things together at the last minute, and it keeps getting worse every week." The idea of blending action and planning, and balancing the spiritual with the practical kept coming up. It was important for nearly everything. I already felt that planning activities were taking a lot of time. Certainly, it was more time than I expected. And here I was again, feeling that I needed another plan. This time it was a teaching plan.

I couldn't keep suffering through this panic. I couldn't stand God's silence when I pleaded with Him. I couldn't disappoint myself or these wonderful people by being unprepared again. I put together a teaching plan for the next year. It seemed daunting at first, but ended up being much more straight-forward than I expected.

The plan would include a mixture of topics and Bible studies. It needed a flow that made sense, and would allow people to keep building on what had been covered before. Of course, if it was a plan, it had to be structured.

The elements of the plan started with an overview of the Bible as a whole. That would be followed by an overview of the Old Testament, and an overview of the New Testament. I had already found some home Bible study materials that would be great for this. Then there was a moment of revelation. The Bible overviews would be followed by a lesson on teaching home Bible studies.

Once I got started, things began to flow. I was really pleased. Compared to the panic I had just experienced, things were greatly improving. I told Ava, "I might have a decent plan after all. This could be really good. With a plan, the church can announce ahead of time what will be taught, and that might attract more visitors. Our people can share with

Panic

potential visitors that we have a plan. Then it occurs to me, people will be more receptive if they know what to expect." Also recognizing the value, Ava said, "Edwin, this plan isn't only good for you; it's better for everyone."

Included next would be a series on the plan of salvation. Clearly, there are particular human acts in that plan. Prior to those lessons, though, would be lessons on grace and faith. After setting the foundation with those, there would be an entire lesson on repentance, followed by a lesson on baptism, and another lesson on being filled with the Holy Spirit. Salvation does not end there, and neither would the lessons. The series would conclude with lessons on a continuing life of holiness and Christian lifestyle.

There would be special events at times. "What about revivals?", Ava asked. I responded, "Let's plan one in the spring and one in the fall. We'll invite an evangelist." We wanted someone focused on people being saved. Each revival would start and end on consecutive weekends. "So", I said, planned revivals will cover four weekends."

By now, we had covered at least 14 weeks. In some of the remaining weeks and at least once each month would be an Old Testament Bible study. These were some of the topics:

Genesis	Job
Exodus	Psalms and Proverbs
Judges	At least two weeks on the major prophets
David's kingdom	
Solomon's kingdom	At least two weeks on the minor prophets
The divided kingdom	

Balancing those Old Testament studies would be New Testament Bible studies. Again, there would be at least one

Panic

each month. These were some of the New Testament topics:

- The birth of Jesus
- John the Baptist
- Jesus' childhood
- Three weeks for the years of Jesus' ministry
  - The year of inauguration
  - The year of popularity
  - The year of opposition
- Palm Sunday would be teaching on the Passion Week and the Crucifixion
- Easter Sunday would include teaching about the Resurrection and the Ascension
- On Pentecost Sunday would be teaching on the outpouring of the Holy Spirit in the Bible
- There would be at least two more weeks on the book of Acts. The first week would address the book of Acts before the missionary journeys. At least one week would address the life of Paul and his missionary journeys.

By this time, the list nearly covered one year. In addition, there would be studies of the epistles by group:

Romans	The Pastoral Epistles
I and II Corinthians	Hebrews
The remaining Soteriological Epistles	The General Epistles
The Christological Epistles	Of course, there would be at least one week to study Revelation.

After coming up with a sufficient list of Bible studies, there were other, mostly broader topics. Some of those topics were:

Witnessing	Bible characters:
Marriage	Adam
Parenting	Noah
The Godhead	Abraham
God's attributes	Moses
Eternity	David
Sin	Isaiah
The Devil	Daniel and the three Hebrew children
Temptation	Peter
Healing	The Disciples
Mercy	The manifestations of God
The Church	
Jewish history	The Sermon in the Mount
Old Testament epiphanies	Jesus' miracles

    It was obvious to Ava that my disposition had improved. She wrapped her arms around me, and with a smile, asked, "So, was this new plan worth it?" Holding that embrace, I said, "This started as a big challenge. It ended up not being that difficult. It was just taking the time to put it all together. Once I started putting it together, I realized there were plenty of things to cover." There were, of course, many more topics and Bible studies that could have been added. I was glad and pleased I had taken the time to do it. I no longer scolded the Lord, "I guess you were speaking to me after all. It just wasn't the answer I was seeking at the time." I think the Lord then said, "That's another topic to add to your list."

    As you could have imagined, there would be adjustments. Things were added. Some things were combined. I would still lean on the leading of the Lord, but at

Panic

least there was a plan to start with. It had more topics than weeks in the year. Some things would obviously carry over into the next year.

I still had to do my own study. The lessons wouldn't prepare themselves. With a plan, though, I could start looking ahead, knowing what the topics would be. I could gather reference materials more efficiently. For the lessons that were series, I could gather material for the series as a whole, and organize it as needed. My workload and responsibility didn't go away, but it became much more bearable.

Feeling so much better, I said, "Now, instead of panic, I have choices." "And I have an amazing husband", Ava said. I couldn't promise that there would be no more panic, but it wouldn't be because I didn't have a teaching plan.

READING GUIDE POINTS:
1. The overwhelming responsibilities during the week leave little time to prepare for weekend services
2. Your family's priority cannot be sacrificed to your ministerial duties
3. When your busyness creates personal panic, God may be silent to teach you a lesson about preparation
4. Anointing isn't automatic; it shouldn't be presumed
5. Planning prevents panic
6. Develop a teaching plan
7. Time spent planning is time well spent

References from:
Effective Christianity: Managing Life's Projects
- Chapter 2, page 13
  - It's not about choosing whether to be practical OR spiritual, it's about choosing to be practical AND spiritual
- Chapter 3, page 18
  - True Christianity requires that we be as effective as possible
- Chapter 3, page 23
  - Part of spiritual maturity is improving how we help others
- Chapter 8, page 76
  - We must manage our time (schedule) as well as we can
- Chapter 8, pages 80-83
  - Following God's direction (timetable) requires that we be obedient, adapt, and endure

Define Your Funnel

Ava has always made wonderful tea. On a hot summer day, a glass of her cold ice tea was so refreshing. In a funny way, making ice tea reminded me of a business process we would apply in reaching out to those hungry souls that were crying for help. For in making ice tea, Ava used a funnel. She would brew the tea on the stove, and then, at just the right time, she would take it off of the hot stove, and pour it into a pitcher or a gallon jug. Steam would rise as she poured the hot liquid into the container. "So how do you know when to pour the tea into the pitcher?", I would ask. "There's no set amount of time", she said. "You can tell when the water's about to come to a boil, and that's the right moment. But if you make the water too hot or leave the tea bags in too long, it won't taste right. You just learn the right way to get it to the point where it's ready."

There was actually a business process used to guide potential customers. Businesses who understood their customers would define what is called a "funnel" as part of their business model. In concept, it was much like the funnel Ava used. I used one too, but it was to change the oil in my car. It was the same principle, but a lot more messy.

A funnel simply acted as a channel. Funnels were usually round, but not always. At the feed store used by farmers, the funnels often had square openings. Nonetheless, the funnel started with a wide opening, and then it would direct or channel what entered it into a smaller area at the exit. Funnels kept things from scattering. The contents going through the funnel could be directed to a specific location. It also prevented things from being wasted.

Define Your Funnel

One summer day, I asked Ava, "So do you really need to use a funnel? Can't you just be careful when you pour?" Her look was odd, but her response was clear, "If I don't use a funnel, the tea will end up all over the kitchen counter and the floor. Instead of tea, we will have a mess." That question would never need to be asked again.

In business, a funnel was used to guide the customer experience. Like the physical funnel, there would be an entry point. From there, though, the process required that you understand your customer and how they thought. Anticipating how the customer would respond to that initial entry point, they would be guided from that entry point to a focused end point. Usually, this would lead to either a sale, a customer contact information, an appointment, or something like that.

Good websites were very good at this. They actually might have many end points. This was especially true for well-planned, customer-based websites. The online process was designed to guide the customer. Even printed materials that were thought out well could be used to guide the customer to a particular end point. There was another term that was more familiar to many. That term was "pipeline".

We needed to do what those customer-focused businesses and good websites were doing. Or maybe there was a more practical example. I joked to Ava, "As a church, maybe we just needed to learn how to make good tea." She replied with a smile, "That's one of the best things you've said all day." Whichever way we needed to think about it, our church needed a funnel too.

There was a young man in our church who agreed to help the church with website development. When I

Define Your Funnel

mentioned funnels, he said, "I've heard about them. Yes, I think that using that concept would be good." With that agreement, I asked him what I thought were good questions. "How can we guide converts, without exploiting them, through this model called a funnel? I've heard about end points. What is our end point? Is there only one?" Then I went further, "Do we understand who our 'customers' are, what they are thinking, and how they will respond?" I felt pretty good, and a little guilty at the same time, for I knew a lot of the credit for my insight was owed to my son, Daniel. At some point, whether by intention or providence, he would get his credit.

    We determined there was more than one end point. Here are the end points we might choose. I remember saying as we started, "Perhaps we can't pursue all of them at once. We need to prioritize. But we can't prioritize them until we define them." Interestingly, we soon realized that websites were only part of it. We documented those end points no matter their application.

    The first end point for our church funnel was to create growth. Looking at it now, the starting point was obvious. But it wasn't obvious until we started writing it down. The developer said, "The starting point in the funnel process is to attract guests, and the website should be designed accordingly." "So, is that the end point?", I asked. "Not quite", he said. "The goal, or end point, is to lead guests to the decision to attend our church." Admittedly, that was the easy point. Remembering that those effective at using funnels had a strong customer focus, we needed to understand the thinking of the unchurched. It came to both of us together, "Understand what an unchurched person is

Define Your Funnel

thinking and what sent them to this website." It wasn't just the website though. "Does our social media direct them to the website? We are supposed to update the church's social media platforms regularly. If we're going to do that, we must define what will draw them to the church website and the church."

Creating growth required that we do more than attract guests. We had to keep them attending after that initial visit. Since we were talking about more than websites, I coveted Ava's perspective. She always saw things that I missed. She said, "When guests arrive, we must be hospitable. Of course, we need to be friendly. That's hospitality 101. But our parking lot, the church entrances, every sign, and every greeter needs to send the message that we are a hospitable church." Again, later, it seemed obvious, but it needed to be said concretely to be part of the plan or the design for our funnel.

Together, we all weren't sure whether the next point was a new end point, or part of the first one. The first end point was to create growth. But once guests realized we were a hospitable church, and continued to attend, they needed to become converts. "I get it now dear", Ava said. "Now I'm seeing how it's working like a funnel". "Wow", I said. "It does work, doesn't it? And it's not complicated. It seems straight forward and rational."

The next rational, natural step in the process was to start home Bible studies. The Bible was still our foundation for everything, including growth. This time, I was the one saying it, "Converts are the result of home Bible studies. We want them to be converted by the Word. Nothing else will sustain revival. We will personally ask people for home Bible studies, but our website should be a key element as well.

Define Your Funnel

Does our website clearly and easily guide them to sign up for home Bible studies? If not, let's change it so that it does."

There were personal elements to the funnel. There was the personal touch they would receive when they visited the church. There would also be the personal touch in asking for home Bible studies. And we would also use evangelists and have revivals. Preaching was personal and the means of reaching lost souls. I reminded Ava, "We already planned for revivals when developing our teaching plan. Now I realize we need it more strongly than ever." Besides, one of our mentors told us, "Church planters usually aren't great evangelists." I had to admit that.

The second, or maybe it was the third, element in our funnel was to make foundational families. If we were effective, we would attract guests, they would return, and they would become converts. So much of what we were pursuing was for evangelism. It was to see people converted. I remembered a great preacher saying one time, "Salvation is for a moment; the making of a saint is the work of a lifetime." An absolutely essential element in what we were to do, whether we called it a funnel, or anything else, was to keep people in the church once they were saved. We had to retain converts. I had to be careful referring to conversion as "only" something. But as vital as conversion was, conversion was not truly an end. It was only a starting point, but a starting point to a beautiful life in Christ.

Our funnel, though, would not treat people as spiritual trophies. To Ava, I again said, "Every convert has a soul. Tracking names and numbers from revivals isn't enough. We must be the church that sustains them for life. We must be with them through each joy and sorrow." "Exactly", she

Define Your Funnel

replied. "They are people, who will become our friends and spiritual partners. Their lives matter."

Ava continued, "This church has what they need. You said that. It's true and it's personal. They need a personal touch from this church." "That's right", I replied. "Being personal means that we will follow up personally with each visitor and each convert. We will get their information. We will text them. We will call them. We will personally visit them."

Ava then asked with a tone of conviction in her voice, "Is that enough? We will see them converted. They will be attending our church. Is that all we need to do?" The answer to that probing question was "NO!"

There was one last end point. It was discipleship. Discipleship will always be the essence of the church. The answer to Ava's question deserved more than one word. With equal conviction, I responded, "No, it isn't enough for people to attend and financially support our church. It is also our responsibility to make disciples of them. They will each have a personal calling. They too will be leaders. It's our responsibility to develop their leadership and help them achieve their calling. It's our responsibility to create a hunger for the Word in them."

Discipleship was so vast. That need could not be met by one method. If our church funnel was to get them to the continuing phase of discipleship, it would require consistent, Bible-based teaching. Material was an essential element of the funnel. I implored, "There has to be discipleship material on our website. The material available on our social media also needs to promote discipleship. What we post will do so. We will encourage our church members to do the same."

Define Your Funnel

We had defined end points. We wanted to guide people to create church growth, to be converted, to become foundational families, and to be disciples. Those seemed like solid objectives certainly. The process had been meaningful and revealing. One fundamental question remained though, "What then is our ultimate goal? What is it not?"

It seemed more important to start by making it clear to ourselves and whomever else that certain things were not our church's intent. Neither our church funnel nor any church goal was financial profit. That wasn't the same as saying that we didn't need money. Having enough money to pay the bills and pursue the conversion of lost souls and their discipleship was important. Yes, the church needed help financially. Honestly, for us personally, finances were difficult. In spite of that, though, I said, not only to Ava, but to Daniel and Mia, who shared in sacrifice, "We're not after their money. We're after their souls. Adamantly holding to that principle is vital. When this becomes about money, the battle is over. We've lost. We will trust the Lord. He will provide through those committed to the Kingdom." To the children, I specifically said, "It's important that you learn this lesson now. Your sacrifice is appreciated. Your mom and I know how you two have given. I pray, though, that this is part of who you are. God calls everyone to sacrifice. It becomes part of us."

More specifically, our goal was not any measure of exploitation. Mia got it. Here's what she said, "Dad, these people we are reaching matter. They are individuals with different personalities and experiences. They are souls with a calling just like us. They are just as important in the body of Christ as I am." As a father, there was no way to describe how happy I was to hear what she said.

Define Your Funnel

Our goals were simple and fundamental. The goal of our church funnel was souls. Our goal in attracting visitors, retaining them, seeing them converted and becoming disciples of Jesus was 100% about their souls. Daniel had helped with some ideas from his business class. I asked of him, "Tell me why we are doing this." His answer was clear and simple, "We want people to be saved. Dad, we want everyone to be saved."

I don't know if it was a different goal, or a restatement of the first, but I felt it was important to say it: "Our goal is spiritual transformation. Purity in our intention is essential. This funnel isn't about manipulation. We are directing them to things transcendent. We want them transformed by the power of the Gospel. Changed lives, and a new, joyous direction is the goal. If we are to guide them, it is commitment to the Kingdom we are after."

Define Your Funnel

READING GUIDE POINTS:
1. Outreach should be intentional; it should guide from initial contact to defined endpoints
2. For outreach to be effective, you must understand how your contacts think and how they will respond
3. Define the endpoints you desire for your converts and design your outreach to get them there
4. The first endpoint is often growth by attracting visitors
5. Other common endpoints are to have return visitors, start Bible studies, create foundational families and establish disciples
6. Connection and relationship are key; your funnel must have personal elements to it
7. The ultimate goal of outreach is spiritual transformation

References from:
Effective Christianity: Managing Life's Projects
- Chapter 7, pages 69-70
  - To define our vision well, we must:
    - Collect requirements or understand what we want to do
    - Define what we will and will not do
    - Control, or stay focused, on what we said we would do
- Chapter 7, page 75
  - A defined funnel is intentional; it prevents distractions

The Juggler

Life was much easier when I could do things one at a time. As a boy, I played a lot of pitch and catch. It started with Nerf balls or things similar. When I got a bit older, the object of choice was a softball. Then when I was a teenager, I graduated to throwing a baseball. One thing stayed the same though. Pitching and catching required hand-eye coordination, but it was focused on just one object at a time.

Juggling, on the other hand, was much different. It required keeping your hands and eyes coordinated on many things at the same time. I tried it once. A boyhood friend was pretty good at it. He said, "Give it a try", and began tossing balls to me. At the third ball, I said, "I think that's enough." He tossed a fourth ball, and it was over.

While watching one thing, if you didn't keep your attention on many other things at the same time, you would "drop the ball". In juggling, nothing was ever stationary. It was all moving at the same time. You didn't dare hold on to anything. If you did, you would drop something else. Like all of these carnival performers who had perfected their skill, the number of things you had to keep from being dropped kept growing. Finally, it became more than one person could manage. One of the balls would hit the floor.

A church planter had to fill many roles. Juggling seemed to be one of them. With a bit of longing, I expressed my feelings to Ava, "I would love to, but I can't focus on one thing. If I pay too much attention to things I like, or even things that are more important, other things don't get done. They get dropped. It seems it will never end. The number of things that must be done, and done well, just keeps growing."

The Juggler

I made a list of things I could think of really quickly that needed to be done. All of them needed to be coordinated. Feeling a bit sorry for myself, I lamented, "I have to juggle all of these things. They have to be juggled. They're balls that I have to keep in the air. This list isn't complete, but here's what I've come up with so far":

- Build a prayer network
- Develop a plan to make connections
- Define strategic goals
- Make decisions about church governance
- Make decisions about church community involvement
- Develop a plan for church operations
- Identify key milestones and high-level activities
- Decide on a launch date
- Decide who should be on the church board
- Come up with a plan for church bylaws
- Translate the long-term plan into goals for the first year
- Develop a schedule, a detailed budget, and charts to track progress
- Review and assess progress
- Adapt all of these plans accordingly
- Create a Launch team
- Create a Core team
- Get volunteer staff
- Ensure legal matters
- Ensure safety compliance
- Make a teaching plan
- Make sure these plans convey our vision and structure for growth
- Establish good at marketing
- Create a good website
- Create compelling social media
- Create an effective email process

The Juggler

- Define something called a funnel, with endpoints
- Manage physical things, like building issues, signs, posters, printing, etc.
- Establish foundational families
- Attract and retain converts

"I know this list will get longer. How am I supposed to juggle all of this?"

I realized I had been here before. I didn't want to be a lone wolf, or captivated by panic. I had learned some lessons.

The first lesson was that I wasn't alone. That was a very long list, but I didn't have to do it all by myself. "Are you putting too much on yourself? Are you trying to be Superman?", Ava asked. She was right. I remembered the story of Moses and his father-in-law. I had no choice but to trust others to help. I would trust their commitment. I would delegate. I, somehow, would let go.

The second lesson was that when you're overwhelmed, practical steps are important. Two foundational practical helps were delegation and planning.

I learned that delegation was essential. If I was going to be effective, and if I was going to keep all of those balls in the air, I couldn't do it all myself. I needed to delegate as much as I could. Then it dawned on me that delegation could be about more than just the tasks themselves. Once I saw that long, unthinkable list of things one person couldn't manage, I began looking for someone else to take ownership for creating the overall plan. I would take responsibility for the content that would be approved, but I needed someone else to help me put it together. That plan would be probably be complete sooner than expected. So, I started thinking about who could the responsibility to track all of the activities and their progress.

The Juggler

Planning was no longer an evil concept. It was an essential ingredient to spiritual success. It was key to preventing panic. I had heard others say, "If you're too busy to plan, then you are planning to not succeed." Someone else said, "If you fail to plan, you plan to fail." I now believed both of those statements were true. I had heard people say, "I don't have the time or money for planning", but they were making excuses and a big mistake. By neglecting to plan, more time and money would be wasted by doing things over. I now professed, "Planning saves time. Planning saves money."

It was human nature to want to get started. People wanted immediate action. I did too. It was usually a mistake. My advice, "Don't just start doing things; plan first." I had already been there. I learned painfully, "Having a plan gives you a calmness in the midst of the unending demands that would otherwise consume you. Chaos is not a solution."

The third lesson was sometimes hard to accept: there's more than one way to get things done. When most jobs were started, there was a sequence to the steps. A person who built schedules for his company told me, "You have to take another look. People who build schedules do it all of the time. Few plans get done on time if everything is done sequentially. A good scheduler looks for things that can be done in parallel. He asks questions. Then when he thinks he's found as much as possible, he has to take another look, and he finds more can be done in parallel than he originally thought."

I needed to listen to other ideas. New ideas might be better. If someone else had a different approach, and was willing to take ownership because I let them do it their way, the job would get done, and I would learn.

The Juggler

'Another way of doing things' included how to manage. Not everything had to be managed the same way. On those long lists of things to do, there were some items that could be managed by one line on a chart. Other items, though, needed their own, detailed plan. That provided opportunity to adapt, and opportunity to delegate. There would be another detailed plan that someone else could own.

Often, it was during these times, that we realized people who we didn't always see as 'strong spiritually' showed us that they were 'spiritual lifesavers'.

Those were nice ideals, but I still had this very long list. I said, "I'm ready to get started." Then I saw that there were so many plans, there was no way I could track each plan separately. I needed to put it all together, into a master tracker. When I told Ava of the tracker, I said, "If I am to juggle everything, then I needed to see all of the balls at the same time if I have any hope of keeping them all in the air."

Ava and I and some key members of the church began meeting to put together this master tracker. One beloved saint said, "Before we start writing things down, shouldn't we decide what the elements of the plan will be?" We prayed for the Lord's guidance. That was followed by a sometimes passionate discussion. But we listened to each other and were able to narrow it down to four elements. I stated our summary conclusion, "So, we're agreed then. The tacker will include tasks, calendar, resources, and progress. Yes?" They all acknowledged their agreement.

With that agreement, we reviewed each plan, and listed every activity and associated tasks we could think of. One of the ladies said, "I participated on one of these kind of exercises on my job. A lot of things will change. The order will

The Juggler

change too. Rather than updating everything on a sheet of paper, I suggest we make it simple and use adhesive notes. Then we can move things as needed, without rewriting everything." 'Fitly framed' came to my mind once again. This simple advice saved us a lot of wasted effort. That was especially true when we started on the calendar.

After coming up with a huge list of activities and tasks, we did our best to put them into a calendar. We kept, as best we could, all of the tasks grouped together that were part of the same activity. It became clear that there were many things that needed to be done at the same time. We discovered what a 'parallel path' was. What was really challenging was deciding what tasks had to be completed for another one to start. It was especially challenging with such a large list of tasks. The scheduler I talked to said these were called "predecessors". Each time we discovered another predecessor, we had to take all of the tasks tied to it, and move them. Ava turned at some point to the precious lady that suggested adhesive notes. "Thank you, sister. I don't see how we could have done this without your suggestion." Everyone in the room confirmed with a hearty "Amen."

Identifying resources for each task was not easy. We had to be 'resourceful', coming up with a growing list of resources. These people would either do the task or take responsibility for it being completed. Quickly we came to a point where we simply didn't have a resource we could identify. One brother sagely said, "We must move on. Let's start with resources on-hand now. When we get to a task where we don't have a resource, we will list it as 'future', or 'to be determined'. But we should also specify which resources are needed now, and which resources we will need later." That was another great idea, but it generated more tasks. We added tasks to identify resources, and put them in the calendar as well. Otherwise, we would forget and run into trouble when those tasks were supposed to start.

We weren't tracking anything if we didn't monitor progress. We needed to know when each task started and when it was completed. For some items, like community involvement, making a decision wasn't enough. We needed to include who would sustain the effort once it was started.

It was important to be honest in tracking progress. As the pastor, it was my responsibility to champion honesty, "We will share honestly with everyone involved the progress we are making. We will show the good and the bad. If things are late, we must admit it. If things cost more than expected, we must admit that too." The real purpose in assessing progress, though, was to make decisions. We had to identify where help was needed.

Some tasks had to be broken down into smaller elements. A number of tasks were longer than a month, and usually, that was too long. We needed to find a way to measure progress quicker. We couldn't afford to wait more than a month to find out we had a problem. We needed to know, and fix it as soon as possible.

Once we started performing all of these tasks, and as we monitored our progress, it became necessary to adapt. We had to make adjustments. We couldn't keep holding on to a plan that wasn't working. We would adapt. Some said that it was a sign of failure to have to change your plan. Others said there was no value in planning if you couldn't follow the plan. Now convinced of the value of planning, I said to the team, "You can't change a plan that you do not have. Without a plan, you have no hope of success."

There was one other key element in our success. Very soon, we got to the point where we had so many adhesive notes and penciled lists that it was getting out of control. Ava encouraged me to consider another approach, "We're drawing lines to connect things, but we don't have paper big enough to connect everything. A kitchen or dining room table isn't big enough anymore. Besides, as soon as we finish a session, everything has to be moved. Whatever room or table we use has other, important purposes." We needed a room devoted to this huge tracker. It was our "war room". One wall became a connected chart, until it too wasn't big enough, and we had to wrap around a corner.

We could add more detail once we had our war room. We had an expected sequence that had been forged with great effort. Yet again there another great suggestion from one of the team members, "We have all of these things in sequence. Let's estimate a duration for each task, the resources involved, and the cost." We did just that. And with that, dates were more realistic. I thanked all of them for their effort. "The juggler now has a complete view of every ball. There is an overall schedule with completion dates. We know when we needed resources. We were able to add up the estimated cost of each activity and task, and compute an overall cost. We added other items that were ongoing costs, such as utilities, rent, insurance, etc. That means we have a reasonable overall budget. You people are amazing." It wasn't terrifying anymore. It was calming. The juggler wasn't alone. There was a team to keep many balls in the air.

In all of the details, it was still important to stay focused on the achievement of fundamental goals. We were tracking many things. Key items, such as visitors, attendance, home Bible studies, would be monitored closely. It was critical to keep track of baptisms and people receiving the Holy Spirit.

We also needed the means to summarize all of these activities. Number of goals achieved and key metrics were established. One of the team members volunteered, "This summary information can be translated into a plan on a graph. We can track results against the summary plan. I'll generate a report, with a chart that shows us our high-level progress." I said, "Yes. That too is amazing, but we still need a war room, where all of the underlying details can be monitored. Without progress there, there will be no progress at all."

There was a myriad of things to do. Of all of the balls that had to stay in the air, many were very spiritual in nature. Things like having a prayer network, seeing people converted and establishing foundational families seemed very spiritual. On that same list, things like bank accounts, church bylaws and safety compliance seemed quite practical. The means by which we would get all of these things done also required a balance of the spiritual and the practical. Ava and I prayed for everything. That was a constant spiritual focus. Then we used adhesive notes to create a plan with a schedule and an overall church budget. Whether it was the content or the method, spiritual and practical things were blended. If we were to be successful, we had to embrace both. How then were we supposed to keep everything in the right balance? Was it by our education, our wisdom or our talent? Quite simply, we needed the leading of the Holy Spirit to keep it all in proper balance. It was no longer a matter of "either/or".

The Juggler

The practical and the spiritual were all essential parts of being spiritual. And this simple truth had not changed: we needed the Holy Spirit to get it right.

I had become a convert of church planning. Once again, I had to make confession to Ava, "What is clear now is that planting a church is a major project. I had no such thought when we started. Coming into this, I was focused on 'spiritual' things. But I've found out there has to be a plan as well. In fact, there isn't just one plan; there are many plans. And all of them have to be managed. Without a plan, planting a church would be overwhelming." Now I saw it. I couldn't imagine how we could succeed without both the leading and prayerful submission to the Holy Spirit, and a plan to accompany that vision. With the help of practical things, planting a church was not overwhelming. But plans were needed, for planting a church was not simple. Planning made complicated things possible.

As we neared completion of the tracker, and with the recognition of the importance of practical things, I felt led of the Lord to tell the team, "Remember, planting a church is primarily a spiritual responsibility. It requires vision, compassion, mercy, and responsibility. It's about redemption, salvation and living in the Spirit. The result we are seeking is souls, souls converted, souls transformed. Where those souls will spend eternity is at stake."

The Juggler

READING GUIDE POINTS:
1. Eventually you will get to the place where you can't do all of the things that need to be done, by yourself
2. You must learn to trust others who want to help you
3. Delegation is essential; it allows you to get things done through others
4. Planning is an essential ingredient to spiritual success
5. Planning makes complicated things possible
6. Accept that there's more than one way to get things done
7. People with strong administrative skills who we don't always see as 'strong spiritually' are often 'spiritual lifesavers'
8. Keep a master tracker of all of your projects, with important dates, responsibility, key resources and costs
9. Track progress honestly
10. Develop a way to summarize progress
11. You will always need the leading of the Holy Spirit to keep things in proper balance
12. Planting a church is a major project
13. Trust, delegation and planning provide the opportunity to track every project, confidence to get more things done, and the ability to stay focused on what' most important

The Juggler

> **References from:**
> ***Effective Christianity: Managing Life's Projects***
> - Chapter 6, page 54
>   - Project management is applicable for spiritual activities and for spiritual people. Effectively managing spiritual projects may require any or all of the following: scope management, schedule management, resource management, and risk management.
>   - Simple project planning tools help achieve great spiritual results
> - Chapter 6, pages 58-59
>   - An effective life in the Spirit requires that we listen to the voice of God, and that we act upon that voice
> - Chapter 6, page 60
>   - True, responsive faith is active
>   - Effective response is coupled with purpose
> - Case study, The Apostles, page 117
>   - The great example of the Apostles shows what great things will be accomplished when the right leadership uses the right processes

Creating a Financial Foundation

A strong church would be built on strong doctrine and strong families. We had committed to that. It seemed like that should have been enough. But it wasn't. There was a third element. It was financial strength. In one of the online videos, it was said, "Spiritual goals depend on financial success. Growth will be hindered, and the church will not be sustained unless it is strong financially." We realized the commitment to doctrine and families should be expanded. Reflecting on this realization, I told Ava, "I'm changing my statement about one of the central points in our vision. Don't worry. I'm definitely not compromising on doctrine. It's a practical addition to our commitment. We are committed to strong doctrine, connected through strong families and sustained by strong finances."

In defense of that statement, I continued, "More churches fail because of financial problems than any other problems. The data shows that all too often, churches that compromise on doctrine and Christian discipline due so because of money. I know that. I have to do my best to prevent us getting to that temptation. My goal is for the church to become strong financially so that there will be no temptation to compromise."

There was another key spiritual principle involved. While compromise could certainly be a temptation, it often was not the first temptation. Often, the biggest and earliest temptation was impatience. A church needed financial discipline. Methods for ensuring discipline were critical. But equally important was the need to wait on the Lord. Our society was driven to succeed, to see results. I was driven to

Creating a Financial Foundation

success and see results. But sometimes the first demand was to wait until His time. Then I could pursue with all diligence. I had already been to this precipice before, when I talked to a property owner about the reason for the failure of the business located on his property. The drive was still in me. I let Ava know that I hadn't forgotten the lesson. "That conversation was pivotal. I learned from that man of the need to control expenses and to throttle ambition. While we were talking, it became clear that it wasn't yet time to get a property. I had to wait until the time was right. If I had been determined to go ahead, it would have been outside of the will of God, and it would have led to financial trouble. It may have led to financial disaster."

Whatever God's timing was for us to follow, one thing I knew. Becoming financially strong was not a fantasy that we would think about at some future date. It had to be a principle that we practiced right away. We needed to begin creating that financial foundation, that path to financial security, from the start.

What would the elements be for a strong financial foundation? Not surprisingly, the key was still our vision, mission and values. As it was with nearly everything, the key was knowing what kind of church we would be. I had just told Ava that financial strength was now a part of our vision. She said, "I definitely understand the financial struggle and sacrifice. We have faced that issue for some time personally. We need to have enough income as a church to pay all of the bills. But how does this 'financial strength' determine what kind of church we will be? Does that mean we are looking for people with money, or at least people who will sacrifice financially?" I had to ponder before answering, "Yes and no.

Creating a Financial Foundation

No, Ava, we're definitely not looking for converts based on how much money they have. Yes, we want members who are willing to sacrifice. I think it's more about our priorities as a church. In clarifying what kind of church we will be, how the church spends its money is part of that. We need to decide what we will support? Giving should be part of our vision."

"The details are important also", I continued. "I learned from the online materials that there are three primary components: financial structure, managing income and managing expenses. We won't be successful unless we deal with all three. It also shows why it's important to have someone who is good at financial management on the team. I certainly don't know how and I'm not able to do all of these things myself."

Structure was the first proof of that last statement. Structure required that we consider operations, income, expenses and giving in deciding how to manage financially. My experience was to set up a bank account and practice discipline in controlling spending. But what I learned from this online material was all the proof I needed to get help somewhere. What made it even more convincing was that what I heard wasn't from a financial manager; it was from a church planter that had been there. He said, "You need to identify income sources and expense accounts separately. Define the purpose of and controls for each financial account. Those things may not be the same for each account." Then he said, "Blend financial management with other financial activities." I saw why it was important, and decided to seek guidance from a financial advisor. I wanted to avoid spending money if I could, but I saw that financially successful people used advisors. And that was true for churches too. An

Creating a Financial Foundation

advisor's perspective would be different, but I had to value that different perspective. I had to listen to their advice.

I had set up my own computer programs to monitor my personal finances in my past. It was evident that would not work now. Besides, that church planter I talked to also strongly recommended that we use good financial management software. "There are many good tools available. Many are quite affordable. There isn't one favorite among churches, but churches are using such software successfully. Another strong point in favor of not doing it yourself is that external software will stay compliant with changes in regulatory requirements and technology."

Budgets were essential of course. Financial targets were important, but they needed to be translated into detailed budgets. This was where the financial advisor helped, "Budgets need to be realistic." They were tight. There wasn't much margin for error, but I thought the estimates were still realistic. He said, "No, it needs to be better than that. You need to have discretionary margins in your budgets, or you will always fall short."

We knew we had to be open about tracking progress. The financial advisor made it clear that we also needed to establish openness in financial reporting, "Data gives you an unemotional view of results. You need to include financial metrics in your reporting. Set them before you need them, or you will be tempted to use metrics that make things look better, rather than tell you honestly how you are doing. Use reports to make sound decisions. One of the biggest downfalls in financial management is refusing to believe the warning signs from financial metrics." One of his most compelling statements was, "I'm fortunate to help many churches. Credible financial systems and credible financial processes are a critical element in the success of churches."

I had heard of maximizing income before, but managing income was different. It was part of the transition from personal income to seeing income from a business perspective. Early on, there wasn't much difference, but that would have to change. There would be refinements later, but as a starting point, we learned it was important to place both income and expenses into categories. All church income would come from some kind of donor. The financial advisor suggested three general categories. "You should target in-house donors, external donors, and online donors. "Place all church income into one of those three categories. Then you need to estimate as part of the budgeting process how much income would be generated for each of those categories." We had an obligation to provide a contribution statement for each donor. The contribution statements needed to be appropriate for the type of business concern they were, and for the donor category. For example, the contribution statement for an individual contributor would probably be different than one for a business contributor. The financial advisor was of great assistance in helping create the accounts for each donor category, and the contribution statements.

The last part of this triad of components was managing expenses. I felt pretty comfortable with this one. I understood categories of expenses. And yes, we had to do that. The financial advisor, again, took it a step further, "You want multiple accounts to manage expenses and how you spend. For operations, you need something liquid, like a checking account. For more determined things, like special projects, you want to limit how easy it is to spend that

Creating a Financial Foundation

money. You should consider separate savings accounts for each special project. This way, your church's savings is not an open checkbook, or a general fund, which are hard to control. Your savings needs to be determined. Another term for this is 'intentional' savings."

We could not talk about having a firm financial foundation without talking about financial independence. Financial strength and financial independence were not exactly the same. Most churches that were planted were probably like us. At first, the church simply could not be financially independent completely. To the contrary, personal finances were very challenging. Ava said, "Financial independence is hard to imagine right now. Some external help will probably be necessary for a while. I don't know how long." By faith, though, I knew that eventually financial strength would lead to financial independence. Like us, every church planter wanted that day to come as soon as possible. I made a bold, 'prophetic' statement, not only to Ava, but to the financial advisor as well. "In looking ahead, seeing the rewards of creating this financial foundation, I announce a target and a goal. We will target a specific date for our financial independence. That's a big reward. Ultimately, though, the goal is more. The goal is to reproduce by supporting others who will also become church planters."

Creating a Financial Foundation

READING GUIDE POINTS:
1. Spiritual goals depend on financial success
2. More churches fail because of financial problems than any other problems
3. One of the biggest and earliest temptations is fiscal impatience
4. Financial strength and giving are important components of a church's vision
5. Primary elements of a firm financial foundation are sound financial structure, and effective management of income and expenses
6. Define the purpose of and controls for each financial account
7. Budgets must be realistic
8. One of the biggest downfalls in financial management is refusing to believe the warning signs from financial metrics
9. For operations, use a checking account
10. Have separate savings accounts for each special project
11. Eventually, financial strength will lead to financial independence

Creating a Financial Foundation

> **References from:**
> ***Effective Christianity: Managing Life's Projects***
> - Chapter 2, page 13
>   - Those who can effectively balance practical matters in spiritual pursuits are the most successful in seeing those pursuits achieved
> - Chapter 6, page 60
>   - Spiritual effectiveness requires response. An effective response includes a plan.
> - Chapter 9, page 83
>   - There is a cost for every resource needed to reach your goal. Every resource, and its cost, must be managed as effectively as possible

Developing Leaders

One of our new members served in the US Army. He told me of 'boot camp', and how difficult it was. But his story included the strength of friendship and the development of leadership, "In boot camp, it was difficult, but you also developed a strong bond with your fellow soldiers. These were the people who might save your life one day, or whose lives you might save. That bond was very strong. Then I was promoted to corporal and sergeant, and I had to learn to be a leader. It wasn't only about friendship at that point. It was also about the decisions I would make as the leader."

Growing up in church wasn't as tough as boot camp, but it was mostly about friends on a personal level. Now so much had changed. I felt I could be honest with this man who had been honest about his own life, "Just like the young man you were, who transitioned from a soldier in boot camp to a leader, possibly in battle, I now am the leader. But it's more than that. It's also my responsibility to develop others into leaders. There will be spiritual battles, and not just for me. These new leaders will have battles too." With a respect he had learned deeply, he said, "I understand that responsibility. I respect and honor your role as leader of this church."

The concept of leadership seemed very personal. It was a personal dynamic. Confronting my responsibility, I told Ava, "It's about potential, energy, human interactions, personality and influence." Showing she understood, she added, "You also want people with great personal skills."

Knowing it was personal, I also professes that I needed a process. "It's just doesn't seem right to approach it analytically. It's doesn't feel like it's about numbers. Yet there are parameters to consider. In fact, when I try to translate all of those personal parameters into some equation, it becomes more than I can handle. Looking at all of the potential leaders any church needs, there needs to be some disciplined process to assure they're all filled, and somehow with the right people. It's not just about individuals. It must be an effective team of compatible resources. Honestly, I'm not sure. Maybe the Bible will give me some ideas on how to balance personal dynamics and the appropriate parameters."

Three leadership teams in the Bible gave me the guidance I needed: Moses and Aaron, Joseph and Pharaoh, and the Apostles.

I first looked at Look at Moses and Aaron. Moses was frightfully aware of his deficiencies. When Moses expressed those leadership fears, God provided a complementary resource in Aaron. He didn't reject Moses; He built a team that was effective. I had to share with Ava my marvel, "Look at how immature Moses was in his behavior and leadership when this started. God gave Moses the resource he needed to take boldness before Pharaoh, and look at all that was accomplished."

Then I studied Joseph and Pharaoh. Pharoah listened when Joseph interpreted his dream. He was a great executive that saw decisive opportunity. Joseph was the perfect administrator to accomplish an amazing plan. Again, to Ava, I exclaimed with wonder the impact of this providential union, "Through this team, the doom foreseen in Pharaoh's dream was transformed into victory. Instead of perishing during great famine, Egypt was prepared, and became great in power."

The third team I studied was the Apostles, and what a

Developing Leaders

compelling example it was. I couldn't imagine a more effective team in the Bible than the team formed by the Apostles. Surely no one expected Paul, this persecutor of the church, to have such a powerful impact in spreading the Gospel of Jesus Christ. Consider, though, the cast of so many, without which, the success of the church would not have been realized. As it was with the preceding examples, I had to share what I was learning with Ava, "Barnabas may have been one of the most overlooked leaders of the early church. It was Barnabas who took Paul under his wings, introduced him to the skeptical Apostles, and journeyed with him to Antioch, and then throughout the first missionary journey. Then there were Silas, Timothy and Titus. They are well-known for their work. But there were so many lesser-known members of the team, like Gaius, Erastus and Epaphras. When you see this as a team, you then see how they all worked together, under the leadership of the Holy Ghost, and transformed Christianity into a movement that reached throughout the Gentile world."

Ava encouraged me, "You said you would go to the Bible to find guidance. I'm sure you made the right choice. Did you find what you needed?" I assured her, "Yes, I did, and now I'm ready to start."

"From what I learned in those examples, I will seek leaders with the following qualities:

- They have to be *accountable*. When they say they will do something, I needed to know I can count on them.
- I will look for people who will **work well with others on a team**. I don't need people who want to be stars. This is going to be a team effort. I need responsible

Developing Leaders

people who will all work together.

There needs to be a ***willingness to learn***. They don't have to be polished. As long as anyone will do their best, work together, and learn, they will be great member of the team.

There also needs to be a ***determination to be better***. This is part of being willing to learn, but it's more than that. Each of us, including me, has to be aware that we can always be better. We are either growing or dying. We will choose to keep growing.

The most important, thing, though, is to ***listen to the Lord***. This applies to me as much as anyone else. There might be people that I don't recognize, but the Lord does. The Apostles were skeptical of Paul. David wasn't the first choice of Jesse's sons. Moses fled from Egypt. Gideon was the least of a poor household. In so many cases in the Bible, God did great things through people that we would have considered unqualified. There might be a Gideon or a Moses in our church that only the Lord knows."

Like almost everything else we had done, there was a practical process to follow. I needed another plan. Selecting leaders would require a staffing plan. The first step in that process was to identify all of the groups in the church that needed leadership. A few of those groups included: Core Team, Launch Team, church board, Sunday School, worship team, musicians/choir, outreach leaders. It was a good starting point. There would likely be many more. Each of them would need leadership. The second step in the process was to develop another schedule. At a high level, I developed a schedule to identify when each team would be needed. Correspondingly then, I determined dates to fill each leadership position. I needed to track progress in filling leadership positions, and make adjustments as necessary.

All of these steps seemed familiar. I told Ava, "I guess I have another project to manage. I cannot pretend this will be any different. Just like all of the other projects involved in planting a church, there will be barriers and challenges. There always are. We can expect them, though, and be determined to get through them. Everything we do has risk. I said 'we'. I also don't pretend that I'm managing all of this by myself. But Ava, with your help, we will manage it. I can't tell you how much you mean to me, and how vital your help is in establishing this church."

Once I had a staffing plan, there were two phases. The first phase was selecting leaders. The second phase was developing leaders. I already had criteria for who to select. I needed to focus on the development part of it as well. I told Ava of the conversation with the US Army veteran. "I am no longer in boot camp. I'm now the sergeant." She suggested, "You might want to change your model, sir. You are at least a captain, maybe a colonel. Edwin, you're in charge." She winked and said, "What are your orders, sir?" As always, Ava made me feel like I was special. But it also seemed even more daunting to consider my responsibility of leadership.

For now, I settled on two things for leadership development: leadership training and regular leadership meetings.

I was confident I could find good leadership training. Our mentors who had done this before would be able to recommend good material. Additionally, there was plenty of good online content.

We will hold regular leadership meetings. The number would grow as more leaders were needed. The mentors and

Developing Leaders

the online veterans all said, "As much as you can, keep these meetings informal. Make sure the content of the meeting is good. They need to know they will be held accountable. However, while accountability is good and even necessary, you and they need to be able to relax and enjoy, not only working together, but being together." I was happy for that advice. It would make things a bit easier. Personally, I looked forward to the informal fellowship.

The plan was only a starting point. We had to keep our eyes open. Developing leaders was an unending responsibility. There would always be a need for new leaders. Thankfully, the Lord was always making others ready to take responsibility. One of my mentors had said, "Some leaders are ready now. Some will be ready later. The work of the Kingdon will be accomplished. God's Kingdom will prosper."

Developing Leaders

READING GUIDE POINTS:
1. As the pastor, your role is that of a leader, more than a friend
2. Leadership is personal
3. You need a disciplined process to fill the leadership positions in your church
4. There are many great examples of leadership teams in the Bible
5. Seek leaders that are accountable, work well with others, have a willingness to learn, are determined to be better, and most of all, that listen to the Lord
6. Treat the task of developing leaders as another project
7. There are two phases to having effective leaders: selection and development
8. Leadership development is structured and ongoing

References from:
Effective Christianity: Managing Life's Projects
- Chapter 9, page 83
  - Be flexible in using project resources
- Chapter 9, pages 83-83
  - Talents must be developed
- Chapter 9, page 88
  - Fulfillment is found through fully expending your talents for the Lord.
- Case study, The Apostles, pages 113-114
  - A case study of the Apostles offers insight into their success and asks questions to consider in developing a team

Finishing the Journey

Creating a Launch Plan

I've felt like many things thus far: coach, juggler, administrator, explorer, missionary, project manager, marketer, and many more. The list was long, and this day, once again, I felt like something new: sailor.

"I had never been a sailor", I said to Ava, "but I feel like one today. I've been pursuing the launching of our church. The whole concept of launching reminds me of sailing."

To launch a ship without preparation and a plan was foolhardy. Especially if it was to be a long journey, or through difficult, dangerous waters. In a very real sense, this was that kind of journey. I had been pursuing my dream and my calling for some time now, and soon I would set sail.

We had only about one year to be ready. I said to Ava, "That may seem like it's still so far away. But all too soon, that day will arrive. Diligence demands that we do our best to prepare." Ava concurred, "If we don't, that date will come too soon."

Getting back to the concept of sailing, it was critical that a ship be strong. Complacency and assumption would not do. Such strength would not be by accident. It would be intentional. There would have to be a plan to get the ship to the condition required to launch.

Without a plan, any unexpected event might force the journey to be abandoned. I couldn't let that happen. It wasn't just the end goal, but the journey itself was a critical part of my calling. I had to keep expressing what was inside my heart to my faithful companion and sojourner, "It hasn't been easy so far, and it won't be any easier going forward. I have to be careful. I have to expect danger. There will be risks. I have to set myself to be prepared for them." The ship had to survive.

A sailor had to set the course. This would not be a casual journey of exploration, to see what would be found in some safe, yet unfocused course. There had to be a known destination, and a determined path to arrive. These things had to be known before launch. I remembered an old saying, "If you don't know where you are going, any path will get you there."

I mentioned that old saying to Ava. She said, "The good thing is we know where we were going. We know the path to get there. We are setting set sail on a determined course."

We already had key things that would guide us. Our vision, mission statement, and core values had been established. They would be the foundation to keep us on course. From the outset, we could and would state clearly what kind of church we would be. We could identify the path we were committed to. It sounded simple, but it was more profound than simple. I told Ava how important values were to me, "We know who we are, and why we exist. Perhaps the most important thing for potential members to know is our values, for that's how they knew how they and those around them will be treated." Ava spoke of how personal this was, "Salvation is personal. The church is personal. Each person must know that they matter."

Fortunately, we weren't the first to be in this position. Many had launched churches. At the dinner table one evening, I said to the family, "Others have taken this journey before us. We will learn from their examples. This is why it was so important to establish a network early. The first step in creating a launch plan will be to talk to that network who have done this before. I already have a list of questions."

Creating a Launch Plan

"What lessons did you learn?"
"What mistakes can we avoid?"
"How did you get help?"
"How did you endure?"

Part of the advice we got from that network was about having a launch team. That advice was, "A critical first step is to identify who will be on the launch team. You need people who are outreach-oriented. They don't all have to be evangelists, but they need to all work together as an effective evangelistic team." One person suggested to us, "People with administrative strength can be important members of an evangelistic team. Again, they don't all have to be evangelists. Even an outreach needs some diversity and balance. These administrative people aren't less important. They will help the team be more successful."

They also told us to set goals for the launch team. Some of the key goals included setting a goal for the launch date, and goals for the number of people contacted, the number of contacts recorded, and the number of people attending church.

Once again, there was a practical side to ensuring success of our church launch and the launch team. There needed to be a budget and a schedule.

There were a number of expenses to prepare for launch and for the launch service itself. Once we had established the launch team, I asked the team leader for an idea of the costs. He said, "All of these things need to be budgeted. There will be costs for the launch facility and decorations. We will need printing and signage for parking and for signs inside of the facility. There will be equipment to rent, and we will need food and supplies. That's the list I have

Creating a Launch Plan

for now. We should probably intend to have some reserve for things we don't know about yet."

I then asked him to put together a schedule. He returned, and told me, "These things will need to be scheduled if we are to be ready on time. We need a contract for the facility, and another contract to either purchase or rent equipment. We need to set a date to start advertising. We should advertise in the local newspaper for sure. But we should also plan on some form of online advertising as well. We need to decide on a date to ensure printing and signs are available on time. And if we're going to have food and supplies for the launch service, we need to set a date for that. And we should also decide when to send invitations for special guests."

We were doing our best to get to financial independence as soon as possible. Selectively, we were still asking for some financial help though. If there was one thing that should be funded, the official launch of our church was it. One of the church planters in our network told us, "Funding must be part of the plan. This is where calling and strategy merge. They work together. It's another one of the ways that the spiritual and practical merge. Your calling is certainly spiritual. Strategy can be more practical." He said, "There's a simple formula for funding. It's just what we're talking about now. Calling plus strategy equals funding. You put the two together, determine how much funding you need, and who will be targeted to help."

I, then, added some items to the team leader's list, "We need to add a target for how much of the expenses will be covered by contributors, a date to start our fundraising, and dates for levels of funding achieved. We will target in-

Creating a Launch Plan

house donors, people who are part of our church now, and external donors. External donors include external people in our network and others in the community. That might be a person or a business. Since we're doing so many things online, we will also find a way to target online donors."

We needed to step up our level of quality. It needed to be appealing to visitors. It needed to be of credible quality for both visitors and potential contributors. Thankfully, the launch team leader didn't need me to tell him that. He told me, "Pastor, this has to be good. Any documentation must be tangible, clear, and of high quality. This is the singular event that will communicate the quality and focus of the church. It must create a good impression." With that passionate plea, I knew I could count on him and his team to deliver well.

There was one last item on the practical side. That was tracking progress. We had said it for all of those items on our master tracker. It was true for this as well. We had to objectively review how we are progressing.

The time was short. That was clear to everyone involved in preparing for this much-awaited milestone. There needed to be a sense of urgency and accountability. There was. From the launch team especially, there was be a commitment of time. I was doing my best to create personal and collective accountability and accountability targets. After a very good meeting with the launch team, I told Ava, "I thought this would take a lot out of me. I'm engaged and taking it seriously. But honestly, I don't have to do much. The team has taken this task seriously. They see it as an opportunity, and have seized it. I don't have to push them hard. My role is to provide whatever support they need." Excitement was in the air.

Creating a Launch Plan

READING GUIDE POINTS:
1. Establish an intentional, determined plan for the official launch of your church
2. Having a launch plan will keep you from being overwhelmed when struggle comes
3. Your launch team needs a balance of evangelism and administration
4. Set goals for the Launch Team
5. Set targets for contributions and fundraising
6. The cost and schedule for launch must be monitored and managed
7. The quality of your church in the community will be exemplified by the quality of the launch service

Creating a Launch Plan

References from:
Effective Christianity: Managing Life's Projects

- Chapter 7, pages 69-70
  - For a project to be managed well, scope must be defined and controlled
- Chapter 7, pages 70-71
  - Vision is the foundation of defining scope
- Chapter 7, page 75
  - There are many distractions to any project. Distractions must be controlled
- Chapter 8, pages 76-78
  - A valid schedule must clearly identify the tasks and their sequence
- Chapter 8, pages 80-82
  - As events reveal God's timetable more clearly, you must continue to be obedient, flexible and determined
- Chapter 8, pages 84-89
  - God has given you resources. Assess, utilize, develop and expend those talents for the Kingdom
- Chapter 10, page 97
  - Even spiritual endeavors have risk. Expect them and manage them
- Case study, Nehemiah, page 108
  - Nehemiah clearly identified the tasks to be performed, who would perform these tasks, and managed continuing risks during project execution

The Launch Location

It started as an exercise to prove our toughness. For reasons that may not have been those intended, it was an experience to remember.

As a boy, we would go to parks and play. In nearly every park, there would be some kind of trail. They were usually in municipal areas, quite easy, well-marked and in open, well-trafficked areas. These trips were inexpensive, safe adventures. Well, that was usually the case.

As a teenager, I went with some friends to a state park that had trails. Some were easy, most were moderate, a few were hard, and there might be one classified as rough. Teenage boys were tough, or at least imagined themselves so, and proved their toughness regularly. I was there with some of my male friends, and we determined we could handle the roughest trail available in this park. It was three miles long, and the description said 'rough'. "Come on, it's only three miles. We can do anything that short. We'll be done in an hour easily", said my friends. "Besides, it's in a park, and you can only go so far." Not wanting to be the coward among the brave, and filled with as much self-confidence as the rest, I replied, "Sure, why not? We didn't come here to be bored. Let's do something challenging. What's life if you don't live it?"

We set out on our short journey, talking of what we would do as soon as we finished. "There's a basketball court, and I brought a basketball", said one. Another suggested, "Does anyone want to try horseback riding? We'll be right by the saddle barn when we finish." That sounded promising. I responded, "I've never been horseback riding. It sounds

The Launch Location

pretty interesting to me."

The trail had some rough spots. There were a few hills that were a little steep, but nothing that any of us would even think of saying were difficult. The trail narrowed a few times, and I was careful to say, "This is the way. It's clearer over here." After a few careful directions, while headed downhill, the trail seemed to end. Going back was not the solution. "Surely, we're almost done", came a voice, suggesting we keep going. We looked in multiple directions, knowing a clearer path was about to emerge. "I think we're lost", came from another voice. "How can you get lost in a state park?", was echoed by most.

"Is anybody there?", was the beacon call from each one of us. Soon, though, we realized, was no one there, and we had better find our way out somehow.

We looked at the sun, but it was near midday. That didn't help. Someone tried to be rational about it, "I'm pretty sure we came from this direction. Let's keep going this way." Without better guidance, we did just that. It seemed like it was a long time. Urgency felt that way.

"Stop! Quiet! I think I hear something!" That voice came surprisingly from someone in the rear rather than the front. Sure enough, there were voices. A family was talking while they shared the outdoors together. I could hear the father say, "No, I think the map says we go this way." Before we had time to cry out, I saw a shirt through the trees. "Look, over there. That must be the trail."

In moments, we were securely back on the well-marked trail. Boasting through obvious ignorance, we almost unanimously claimed, "I told you. We put ourselves right where we needed to be." As soon as we were on the trail, we

The Launch Location

saw the signs for the trail head. In a few minutes more, we were resting in a shelter, talking of this great experience.

Privately, being more honest, it seemed natural to say, "I wish we hadn't made that wrong turn. We would have stayed on track, and we would already be on horseback." But if that were so, I probably wouldn't remember this story so well. The difficulty we experienced is what I remembered most.

I've had been on this church planting journey for more than four years by this point. It has been a great experience, but it hasn't always been easy. There have been struggles for sure. But there has been great triumph as well.

Struggle was dwarfed by those great arisings in my heart. My call was certain, and my foundation sure. There was a growing sense of compassion and mercy. A consuming responsibility had arisen in our family and in a nucleus of wonderful people that I would have never known had I not accepted this call. I had developed many plans and created teams that had learned to work together in the work of the Kingdom. There was a call of the lost who I knew in my heart would find hope, and that call screamed ever louder as we neared this great milestone. A sense of urgency was heightened with every day that passed.

So many times, it seemed like it was taking forever. Multiple times, I had said to Ava, "The path seems so slow, and the progress is halting." It was like that point when the trail ended. But now that we were almost there, my tune had changed, "Now, it seems like it has only been a short while. We're almost there." Her heartfelt response was, "Yes, dear. I can feel it so close. It's hard to imagine where we are now."

We weren't quite there yet, but I was already looking

The Launch Location

in retrospect, "Do I regret the journey? Do I regret the challenges? Would I rather we had taken all of the right steps, and avoided mistakes? Would I wish that it had been easy?" If I wasn't the one in the midst of the battle, or if I were the one planning this course for myself or someone else, I would have chosen the path of ease. I would have chosen to avoid all of the mistakes. But that was not my answer. In prayer, I told the Lord, "No, as it was on the trail in the park, overcoming the challenges has been one of the most important parts of the journey. I wouldn't change anything." I felt the Lord speak to me, "I brought you through the challenge. Struggle will make you cherish it more. Your testimony will be more powerful to those who follow your example."

How could it be? I was refreshed and renewed. My energy was not depleted. There was a new energy to finish the last leg of this important race. We were nearly there.

In just six months, we would launch a church in this city. We had a plan. All of the planning had built to bring us to this point. At some point, though, the plan had to be replaced with execution. Now was that time.

That is not to say that the plan and planning no longer mattered. They certainly did. Excellence had been the foundation of the plan from the beginning. I felt led to pen these words that would be shared many times, "Just getting something done will not be enough. We, as a church, will not accept just anything. After all of this work, all of the commitment from so many great people, and the tremendous vision that has evolved on this journey, we are determined to execute this plan with excellence."

The next step was to choose an excellent location for launch.

The Launch Location

A few months back, I had met an owner of a property that was vacant. The previous tenant business had started well. Unfortunately, they expanded beyond their means, began to struggle, and eventually had to close. It was an unfortunate result, and served as a good lesson as we moved forward. I went back to this property owner, and asked him about the status of the property. He said, "It's still vacant." That seemed like good news. But as he explained further, the news wasn't as good as it seemed, "To keep my operating costs to a minimum while ensuring the building will at some time be habitable, most of the utilities have been turned off. There has been no upkeep of the building. There has been some vandalism that we can deal with when there is a viable tenant." That was a point where determined faith and obedient objectivity had to merge. I had to tell the owner, "I'm sorry. We can't bear our part of the cost of rehabilitating the building, especially for a single event." What I had hoped would be promising opportunity, we had to abandon. We were back at the start, looking for the right location.

We were willing to be flexible. We considered churches, schools and event centers. We even considered warehouses. Our mentors had advised, "Best practice is to choose a location carefully, making sure the reputation of the property matches the character of our church. Amenities like parking, care and activities for children, and ample and accessible restrooms are essential. Safety has to be taken seriously." They also stressed firmly, "While reputation and character are paramount, you cannot overextend yourself financially and put the church in an unstable position at the outset, or launch." So, it became challenging. A couple of times we thought we were close, and another lesson proved

The Launch Location

true. I remembered the voice of one of those mentors, "Expect rejections. Keep moving forward when they come. Do your best to be creative and innovative. Exhaust all options that you can imagine." The advice we had hoped would be unnecessary was holding true. The launch team was fully engaged. Other church leaders were included in discussions about how we were (or were not) progressing.

This was another venture and challenge of faith. While fighting within myself to stay encouraged, I exhorted the launch team, "We are not giving up. We've prayed. Then we prayed more. And we will pray again. If we can't do anything else, we will pray. Prayer will see results." "Jesus", I said, "let these words be true."

There was a turning point one afternoon. There had been no special attention that day. It was the same abiding concern (or was it determination?) that we knew the day before. And the day before that. For all of us, it had been many days before. One of the launch team members had an idea, "I don't know if it would work. At the same time, I don't know why I hadn't thought of it before. I work for a consulting company. As part of our consulting services, we have a training center. It seats at least 100, there is some expansion capability, and it has a small platform, and a few small classrooms. They have some sound equipment and a projection system for training presentations. My company isn't huge. I can probably find out who is responsible for the training center." Maybe, just maybe there was hope.

It took a couple of days for him to talk with the training program manager, but in a few days the promise grew stronger. "Yes, they do allow other groups to use the facility. It doesn't happen often, but they even have a fee structure to

The Launch Location

use the facility." But what he said next was even more promising, "They want to make a positive contribution to the community, and prefer that the facility be used for charitable purposes. To support that, they have a reduced fee structure for charitable groups to use it. Because of our involvement in the community, they already know about us, and we would qualify for the reduced fees." Hallelujah!

The launch team member set up a meeting with the training center manager. We discussed dates the facility could be available, settled on a date, and came to an agreement. The manager said, "We don't have any other plans for the facility that weekend. So, we can give you access to the facility beginning Friday evening. We don't need any extra money since the event itself is only one day. Since your point of contact is an employee of the company, he can take responsibility for security, and work with the training center staff to find out about operation of the facility."

Our hope was to find a facility that would be donated, but the Lord had another plan. As a new, and as yet, unlaunched church, we wanted to keep every expense to a minimum. However, when we looked at God's answer, we were thankful. We had a wonderful facility with a respected, established organization. It was in an area that was safe and of good reputation.

I explained to the people we were already meeting with, "Really, everything we truly need is provided. Restrooms, parking, equipment, and the opportunity to place proper signage are all provided." When these faithful people who we loved and had learned to trust heard the story, they quickly and happily gave. Coupled with those tremendous partners who had been there from the beginning, it was

The Launch Location

enough to meet the financial need. We had cried together may times before. This time, we cried with our hands raised, and joy that was overwhelming. This was the first crucial step in executing the launch plan. The excellence for which we had prayed had been realized, and we knew we were going to enjoy a great, momentous start to this long-awaited vision. A church would be planted in this city.

READING GUIDE POINTS:
1. As you near the date for church launch, what has seemed to take so long will now seem so sudden
2. As you near this milestone, you will not regret the challenges you have faced
3. Overcoming challenges is one of the most important parts of the journey
4. Keep striving for excellence as you select the location for your launch
5. Don't let rejection discourage you; expect it
6. Be disciplined financially; don't launch your church in a bad financial position
7. Continue to trust the Lord to provide the right opportunity

The Launch Location

> **References from:**
> ***Effective Christianity: Managing Life's Projects***
> - Chapters 7, page 75
>   - The drive to achieve your dream compels you to endure
> - Chapters 7, pages 110-117
>   - For our visions to be realized, it is critical that they be clearly defined
> - Chapter 8, pages 80-82
>   - Responding in the Spirit requires both obedience and flexibility
> - Chapter 10, page 95
>   - Whether things go well or trouble comes, you must continue by faith
> - Case study, Parking lot, page 116
>   - Listening and considering other approaches is often a key component in success

The Launch Service

I wasn't always the best student in math and science. For some reason, though, I was just naturally gifted in spelling. My parents recognized this, and, in the fourth grade encouraged me to enter the spelling bee at school. I said, "Sure." I told my teacher, and she was very encouraging. That's what teachers do you know. She told me, "I'm sure you will do well." I wasn't really all that interested. In fact, I nearly forgot all about it, until the night before the spelling bee. My mother asked me if I was ready, and I said, "I guess." The truth was I hadn't put any effort or study into it. It was just spelling. You either could or you couldn't. So, we went through a list of words, and a few students misspelled right away, and were dismissed. The pace of dismissals slowed, and eventually there were only two of us left. I thought that was pretty cool. I knew I would be the spelling champion. My confidence was high.

The word was "indigenous". I had heard of it, but didn't really know what it meant. However, my skill had gotten me this far, and I was still confident of my phonetic prowess. "I-N-D-I-G-I-N-O-U-S". I replied, and smiled with confidence. "That is not correct", said the moderator. The other student was given their chance. "I-N-D-I-G-E-N-O-U-S", they recited. "That is correct", said the moderator. And with one more correct spelling by my "opponent", I was the runner-up.

Since I hadn't given it that much thought, I should have been unfazed. But then it hit me, "I was so close to being the champion." Most would have been thrilled to be the runner-up. It was something to boast of, I suppose, but there was something that lingered in me, "What if I had tried harder? Would I be the champion if I had taken things just a bit more seriously?"

My parents didn't miss the chance to tell me, "We hope you learned a lesson about being responsible." They were right of course. But they didn't need to tell me. The lesson had been learned very well.

Next year, as a fifth grader, it was different. I did take it seriously. Thinking ahead, I remembered how close I had been. And there was only one chance. There are some things where you don't get a second chance. The dream would be achieved, or that dream would be dashed, based on what happened on one day. This time I was more nervous. This time I cared. I had a dream. No one had to remind me. "Today is the day", repeated uncontrollably in my mind. As it was last year, it was narrowed to just two. I had the chance to do well. Yes, I knew it was about doing my best. But I knew my best was to be the best. The other student misspelled a word, and I was able to spell it correctly. There was just one word left, and I would be the champion. The word was 'quarrelling'. It seemed simple now. As I thought carefully, I began to recite, "Q-U-A-R". Oh no! I wasn't sure. My mind was racing, "How many 'R's, and how many 'L's, are there? Is it two 'R's, or two 'L's? Or is it two of each?" I had to finish. I had started, and couldn't stop now. With apprehension, I said "R". Then "E-L". In my mind, I said, "Here goes. It's now or never." This was the moment. To win, I had to face the pressure of the contest. Only those who pushed themselves to that point could learn that lesson. "L-I-N-G". "Quarrelling", I repeated with all of the trepidation I could handle as a fifth grader. It seemed like it took forever, but it was only a

The Launch Service

moment. "That is correct", said the moderator. And with that, it was over. My victory was decreed, "You are the champion." I wasn't the quarterback of a football team, or a great pitcher in baseball. That would be someone else's glory. But I had done it. I had faced the challenge that would be realized or be ever so close as a result of one event.

I was reminded of that pressure and victory as we prepared for the launch service. Achievement, struggle, performance. The importance of these things was on my mind continually. We had been planning. We had been anticipating for so long. I was back in the spelling bee. There would only be one chance. It was a milestone that marked the capstone of our calling. We had awaited this event. And it would be here so very soon.

Consumed as I was, I had to rejoice, "Thank you Lord! You have blessed us with some wonderful, devoted people that are the nucleus to move forward. We have talked with mentors who have done this before, and we will do our best to follow all of their advice. We are so grateful for our church family, and those who have contributed anything to help us on this journey. The date is set. It's about to happen. You have also blessed us with a great location for the launch. We have a budget for advertising, and community awareness. We are putting all of these plans in motion."

Things were coming together. Through the launch team member that was employed by the host consulting company, we were able to gain early access, and learn how to operate the equipment at the training center that would be the site of our launch. Good signage was important. One of the ladies on the launch team had contact with a company that would give us a good price for high quality signs for the

The Launch Service

event. She told us, "There's a schedule, and I'm staying in contact to be sure it stays on schedule." That was nailed down. It was one less item to worry about.

It seems there were only two things left, but they were very important. We needed to plan the actual launch service, and plan for follow-up.

One of the leaders we chose with great prayer was the worship leader. Praying together, we decided, "Let's go ahead and plan what songs we will sing, and how much time we should expect for worship." There would be an outside minister to serve as master of ceremonies. He would keep the service moving along, and start the service with prayer. I urged the team, "I want to give thanks to you, our launch team, and welcome all visitors. We should also acknowledge special guests." Invitations were being prepared, and we were praying for a good response. In concert with our proclaimed church values, the theme of the service would be "Examples of Christ in the Community". I didn't always announce sermon titles ahead of time, but for this, I hedged a bit, "I am choosing a title that aligns with that theme."

Preparing for the service included practicing. We had already started practicing the order of service, and as we were warned, some corrections were needed. We would have a practice run with the out-of-town moderator on Saturday. I was pretty sure we had gotten most of what we needed, but there was always the question, "What are we forgetting?" Just like the lesson from the spelling bee back in fifth grade, there was only one chance to do this right. We were doing our best to have a service that represented excellence. Excellence that was recognized by the community, yes. But a devotion to excellence that honored

The Launch Service

our Lord was most important.

This might all have been in vain if we didn't plan for follow-up. While giving attention to every detail for the launch service, we needed to plan for what would follow. After the momentous event, we could not afford a letdown. I instructed the team, "We have to be prepared for week two." I really wanted to dismiss the launch team as soon as possible, and say that their excellent work was finished as soon as the launch service was concluded. The fact was we don't have enough resources to let them go quite that quickly. I urged them to continue, "We will need your help for at least a short while during the follow-up."

One of the team members had completed a form to collect visitor information as easily as possible. She had done more, saying, "A page has been developed to allow visitors to contact us through our website. Verbiage has been developed for a social media page that will link them to secure sites, like our website. We want to be careful not to put people at risk by putting too much personal information on a social media site." All paper forms, and website or social media would provide information to contact the church. We set a deadline of 30 days after launch for follow-up from the launch team. After that, we had to move to a new, ongoing phase of gathering visitor information. Collecting visitor information would no longer be an event. It would be part of our process.

Thankfully, we were very busy. Being consumed with all of the duties and planning almost allowed us to be worry-free. Well, almost. We were all a bit nervous, but doing our very best. There were persistent comments, "We're getting so close, and look at all that still has to be done." But there

The Launch Service

was no complaining. The team was positive throughout. It had to be the Lord that sustained us. It was His calling and His presence that renewed us. People had worked hard, and they deserved both recognition and rest. It was now so soon.

And then, suddenly it seemed, it was time. Friday evening arrived. It was time to do all of the work to get the training center ready. Signs were placed. We practiced. Our master of ceremonies was remarkable. He cleared duties from his schedule to ensure he was there on Friday evening. His calmness and maturity during our frantic preparation proved that God had directed us to the right partner in this long-awaited day. Saturday's "dress rehearsal" started with prayer. The rehearsal helped a great deal. There were some issues, and questions of "Now what?" But people kept their composure, and we trusted that if we were doing our best, God would take care of our shortcomings.

Honestly, Saturday night wasn't terrible, but it wasn't easy either. I was still asking myself, "What have I missed?" I found later that this was a common issue for nearly every member of the launch team. We all wanted it to go well.

As we gathered on Sunday, a special presence overshadowed. It was a presence we had experienced often. The Holy Ghost was with us. The service began well. The introductions were done. Equipment was adjusted as necessary. The worship leader led us in a mixture of old and new Pentecostal songs. There was nervousness as visitors tried to figure out how to respond to a form of demonstration in worship that some had not experienced before. We had prayed for the Lord to have His way in the service. We had talked about this. "We will not 'force' a particular outcome, but be ready to let the Lord take over if

The Launch Service

He chooses. We've trusted Him so far; we have to trust Him now." It was clear that the worship and the Word touched their hearts. Afterwards, a few came and asked, "You talked about baptism in the name of Jesus. It touched me. Can I be baptized?" Without hesitation, we took steps to make that happen. The message on being examples of Christ in the community must have been the leading of the Lord as well. Many visitors said to me, "We would love to be involved in this kind of church." Other representatives from the community said, "We welcome your presence in the city, and look forward to working with you."

Finally, it was over. It went well. What started as a hug with Ava soon became a group hug with the entire team. It was coupled with tears of joy. The only words I could find through my tears were, "All of your effort, your anxiety, and the prayers you offered were worth it. Oh, praise the Lord!" His presence moved us as our hearts resounded in collective praise.

We could have second-guessed what happened, and what could have been better, but none of that mattered. The time to celebrate had come. The follow-up was on. The church was launched. A new era was beginning.

The Launch Service

READING GUIDE POINTS:
1. There is only one chance to demonstrate the excellence of your church in the launch
2. The launch service spurs excited anticipation for you and the launch team
3. The launch service is a great opportunity to be grateful for all that helped you get to this milestone
4. Devote lots of planning and practice for the launch service
5. Plan ahead for follow-up and what you will do after the launch service
6. Prepare well, then trust the Lord for His will in the service

The Launch Service

> **References from:**
> ***Effective Christianity: Managing Life's Projects***
> - Chapters 7, page 71
>   - The scope of spiritual projects must be controlled. Visions need to be clearly defined, and their purpose realized
>   - As certainly as we know He filled us with His Spirit, we know His voice as it directs us to His calling in us
> - Chapters 7, page 73
>   - Effective decisions require good information. More importantly, there must be an atmosphere of honesty, integrity and trust
> - Chapter 8, page 82
>   - Every great spiritual work is challenged. When the project is complete, we are amazed and fulfilled, and our faith in Him is assured.
> - Chapter 10, page 90
>   - Faith accepts risk, prepares for it and alleviates the associated fear
> - Case study, Church Dinner, page 116
>   - Dealing with problems does not mean a project failed
>   - Often, it is the determined followers who ensure success

Transition

My testimony was unusual. I suppose being unusual should have been expected. I was always 'The Pentecostal Oddball'. Even my experience receiving the Holy Ghost was different. I told this great story, my testimony, to my children. "I did not receive the Holy Ghost in a church. As a pre-teen, I received the Holy Ghost in someone's living room. My family was in the home of a couple who would eventually become strong members of our church. That day had not yet arrived, but it would be very soon. My parents prayed for this lady, and in her living room, she was filled with the Spirit. Moments later, their attention shifted. They saw me praying. So quickly, and so assuredly, I was also filled with the Spirt in what was for both of us a sacred place, a living room."

I had never heard anyone else testify in this fashion, so again, the experience was unusual. The story continued. "The next morning, I felt different. Yes, the moment of receiving the Spirit was inexplicably transforming. That abiding assurance would be with me through every mountain and every valley. But the next morning, as I awoke, I realized, 'This is the first day I awoke filled with the Spirit.' I went to school that day knowing my life was different. There was a newness that was more than a moment of emotional ecstasy. It was a new life."

Testimonies varied in detail. Some may have seemed unusual, but one thing I believed was constant. In fact, I preached about this. "Everyone who is filled with the Holy Ghost knows the indescribable feeling that comes at that moment. It is just that – indescribable. To those who have not had that experience or doubt its importance, or even its

Transition

necessity, we do our best to explain. But our words fail. If only we could be more effective in breaking through, to get people to know what we know, their doubts and rejection would melt away. The magnificence of His presence is transcendent. We do our best, and we cannot explain, but it will transform you."

Those who received the holy Ghost knew it is difficult, and even dangerous, to liken it to anything else. In fact, "There is nothing else like it", was often the only way it could have been described. With that said, and at the risk of seeming profane, the next day after our launch service was somewhat like that first morning I awakened after receiving the Holy Ghost. A church had been launched in our city. The first thing I said to Ava the next morning was, "It's actually happened. We are no longer hoping to become a church; WE ARE A CHURCH!"

We were in a new phase, transition. All of those things we had learned to that point had helped us. It wasn't just about having services and preaching, although that would still be central to what we were and what we did. There were still so many things to plan and manage. It was much like a new convert striving for discipleship and becoming more like our Lord. In that sense, we had only just begun.

Then it was as though a fresh anointing fell upon me. Maybe it was a carryover from the anointing that had been upon us the day before, in our launch service. I tried to capture a vision of where we were on paper. After a short while, I can't know how long, I recited it to Ava. "We still need teaching plans and strong, foundation families. We must continue to be intentional in planning involvement in our community and outreach. We must be united in our

Transition

vision, vessels of mercy, and examples of responsibility. There must be a passion for the lost and a sensitive, effective response to the call of the hungry. We have a long-term plan; it needs to be followed and adapted as His work unfolds before us. We need teams and devoted leaders. Leadership is not fixed; it is evolving, dynamic and ongoing. We must couple spiritual passion and administrative skill. For that, we must recognize each other, our strengths and the value of each one to the Kingdom. We must remain vibrant in the Spirit and its demonstration. We must, at the same time, manage and administer the practical aspects of this spiritual work to which we are called. In that same sense, our firm foundation of doctrine must be coupled with a sure financial foundation. Exuberant faith must be balanced with wisdom and sound judgment. An effective church is credible in its community." Refreshed and exhausted at the same time, I stopped. "Where did all of that come from?", Ava asked. "All of what you said is true. It almost sounded like prophecy. If we can do what the Lord just gave you, this church will be a great church."

"Yes", I said. "That sounds really good. It describes the character of a great church. Still, the launch service was only the start of some practical things that must happen. We went from Bible studies in homes to small group meetings. Some of those places became preaching points. Now we have launched. That's not the end though. Our plan assuredly is to become self-sustaining, self-governing and self-supporting. That's essential. To do that, we must find a permanent location. The launch service has opened doors to people who will welcome our place in this community. We have explored some locations already, and we must pray for the Lord to

Transition

guide us to the place that will become a spiritual landmark. It will become a landmark to many new souls. In the Spirit, I see a reach even beyond this city. My goal is for this to be the place that will fuel others with like calling."

There seemed to be a puzzled look on Ava's face. There were a few moments of silence. Before I could frame a question, she spoke, "I still believe everything you said. It's hard for me to grasp all of that right now. So much of it sounds far away. Where do we start? What do I focus my prayers on now?"

"I don't know how soon it will happen", I answered. "We don't want to get ahead of God's timing, nor can we be complacent. So, the next big milestone to pray about is finding a permanent location. I'm counting on you. If you feel checked in the Spirit, I need to know that. But as soon as we know it's time, we need to take action. Ask the Lord to guide us to the right people and the right place. I will ask everyone who is involved in our church to join in that prayer."

I then got very practical, "Let's be realistic. We need all of the help we can get." Ava smiled. Those had been her exact words many times. I then added some specifics to my realism, "Money is an uncomfortable subject, but I can't afford to ignore the issue. I want to take advantage of help that's available. In North American Missions (NAM), there are sources of aid to help purchase property, and even to help with personal expenses. I'm not too proud to admit I can use that kind of help. There is a Christman for Christ (CFC) fund to help North American missionaries. Our church -- yes, I can now say, OUR CHURCH -- is a prime candidate for that support. We're not there yet, but I pray it won't be long, until we have a youth ministry. Young people need focus and activity. Community is vital to their spiritual existence. There is a Move the Mission fund to help new, small churches with youth ministry. I want to be ready to use that help as soon as we can." Ava's response was short, "Oh, that would help so much. The sooner, the better." I proclaimed, "One day, we will no longer need assistance, and will support and rejoice with others who will benefit from it. But today is not that day."

I moved to the next prayer need. "Keeping things practical, remember the 'cement of administration'. I'm going to need some help with all of this administrative responsibility. So, pray for people who can help with that. Applications must be completed and submitted properly. Follow-up and clarification must be timely. Deadlines must be met. Thankfully, there are great members of the church who are willing to help. Pray that they are available. If you can, please think of a team we could form to help with applications and administration." "I'll come up with something", Ava said. "I'm thankful such help exists. I don't want to miss any opportunity."

"There's one more thing we should start praying about now", I said. "Yes, finding a permanent location is a central need now, or soon. But there is another key milestone. It's probably after we get a permanent location, but before we realize it, we will be looking for formal, organizational approval of our church within our district. Let's confirm what all of the steps are. Pray we don't miss anything. I know there must be a formal application for recognition. I'm pretty sure a meeting must then be scheduled with the District Board for approval. There are only certain times on the calendar that can be done." "What's that like? Are there lots of questions?", Ava asked. "It sounds a little intimidating." "Oh" I replied, "It needs to be taken seriously. There will probably be questions accompanied with maybe some direction and other wise counsel. Truthfully, though, what else would we want? We intend to be a successful part of this district. We want the District Board to care enough to know us and to provide wise direction. Their leadership is vital to our ongoing success." "OK", she said. "I just hope it's you answering the questions."

Yes, this was a great, new day. Launch was behind us. We were transitioning to more. It would not be immediate. We would have to be happy with each step forward, as small as it might be. But in this moment, I remembered how we started. To Ava, I asked, "Do you remember not so long ago, dear? There were questions, concerns, and even doubts. It was sometimes a nervous journey of faith." "Yes", she said. "But through it all, there has been peace." "I agree", I said. "I've had a certain confidence and direction. This truly is the work of the Lord, and I'm amazed and overjoyed that He has brought us to this place." As it was with all who were willing to accept the call, to see the fulfillment of this dream was more satisfying than any human accomplishment. To fulfill His will was more important than anything else. There was still much to do as the journey continued to unfold. Praise the Lord! I wanted to testify again, but with a new, dawning excitement, "Yesterday, I said, 'A new era is beginning.' Today, a new era has begun."

Transition

READING GUIDE POINTS:
1. Once the launch service is complete, a realization dawns that you are no longer planning to become a church; you are a church
2. Rejoice in achieving this milestone
3. This key milestone creates a new sense of excitement, birth and anointing
4. Your church is now in a transition from infancy to maturity and independence
5. It is now time to implement all of the plans for a Core Team, staff, and church administration
6. Take advantage of every opportunity for financial support
7. Acquiring a permanent location is important. Wait on the Lord for His direction and timing, then act when He leads.

References from:
Effective Christianity: Managing Life's Projects
- Chapter 7, page 69
  - Success is unlikely unless the requirements are known clearly
- Chapter 7, page 70
  - For our visions to be realized, it is critical that they be clearly defined
- Chapter 7, page 71
  - Knowing brings responsibility
- Case study, Nehemiah, page 115
  - The leader cannot do everything. Both the responsibility and the success are shared.

The Juggler – Reprise

I didn't ask for this. Tangibly, what we sought had been realized. The intangible, though, was a great surprise. I expressed amazement to Ava, "I could not have imagined all of the tremendous, intangible things that have happened. I saw ahead of a building, a congregation, and other things we would see. Not only did I not pray for these unseen things, I couldn't have imagined how to say that prayer." She replied, "Only those who have gone through this can understand what you just said. To be honest, if I had known what to pray, I would have been afraid to ask for it."

I had learned so much. "That's what I mean", I said. "Learning is one of those intangibles. It's characterized in many ways, but you can't touch it. Truly, though, what an amazing learning process this journey has been. Looking back at my intentions and goals, I don't think I would have said, 'I'm doing this because I want to learn as much as I can'." Two things immediately came to mind from that statement: mistakes and trials. Continuing, I said, "For me to say, I wanted to learn, almost certainly meant that I wanted to make mistakes. Why? Mistakes are what taught me best. Formal education is important of course. Sadly, I have forgotten much of what I learned through formal education. But when people learn from mistakes, there's usually some price paid, and that lesson isn't forgotten."

The price of making mistakes was often the seed and the substance of trials that would come. Some trials were completely external. They were not of my own doing necessarily. "But", I confessed, "many trials are, in some way, a result of some mistake, or a reflection of weaknesses and

The Juggler - Reprise

shortcomings in our character." If I wanted to excel and to lead, those character lessons were necessary. I didn't enjoy those lessons. I'm sure I wouldn't have sought them. What I was seeking was about my calling, and achieving a specific result. That result was the vision we saw: a church planted in this city. But learning was part of it.

Learning was the substance of my growth. I could see it afterwards. Those who go through trials learn much from them. Few, afterwards, regret the trial. In the trial, the growth is not apparent. It is the struggle that draws our attention. As so many great mentors have said, I now echo, "I'm thankful. I'm thankful that the Lord has given me the opportunity to take His challenge, to fulfill His calling, and to see how I have grown in Him, and because of Him."

First, and most importantly, I learned many spiritual things. My faith was stronger. It wasn't just an intellectual belief that I had about Him; it was a faith coupled with action and results. I had seen Him move. He moved in me; he moved in others. I wanted to be sure my children understood this. I told them often, "I've learned to believe in others. You can truly count on people whose lives are filled with the Spirit. To give attention to those who disappoint us is the wrong focus. There are so many people that have been faithful. God is faithful, and so are His people."

I learned that His Word was powerful. To plant a church, you had to trust in the Word of God. We focused on Home Bible studies. We taught the Bible. We preached the Bible. My encouragement to anyone wanting to plant a church was this, "If you trust in that simple focus, it will have results. Focus on the Word of God. It is still His Word that changes people's lives."

The Juggler - Reprise

I also learned many practical things. Spiritual success was a balance of the practical and the spiritual. I was now convinced of that. With that conviction, I often said, "You cannot truly say you are spiritual without both. If you say you are spiritual, and neglect basic, practical things, you become like the person in the Parable of the Talents that wasted His one talent. Our Master expects us to be effective."

These simple things I had learned had given me a new confidence. To our small, but growing congregation, I proclaimed boldly, "I believe God will continue what He has begun. With His help, we will succeed. God will succeed. There is no denying that. Nothing will stop His will from being accomplished. My personal determination, and I hope it is yours, is to stay in His will. For it is there that we will succeed."

A new story was being told again. It was the story of the juggler.

It was like a play with a second act. The structure and components of the story were the same, but the details were a bit different. Though much of it seemed the same, it felt new nonetheless. The context, this 'new world', this second act, was different.

How was it the same? I told Ava, this time with more confidence, "Just as before, there are too many things to juggle at one time. My duty is still like a juggler's, to keep my hands and eyes coordinated on many things at the same time."

"I've learned to be more comfortable. If I watch only one thing, I will drop something else. I learned that lesson the hard way. Everything is still moving at the same time. The number of things that have to be managed keep growing."

The Juggler - Reprise

"The Lord has taught me not to panic. I can't be a lone wolf. Doing it all by myself will lead to panic, collapse and failure. I must trust others. I have learned that I can."

"I have learned to be more flexible, and to be willing to learn from others. I'm not always the teacher. People have surprised me. Those who I thought weren't spiritually 'strong' proved differently."

"We've both grown a lot, dear", Ava said. "You're so much calmer. You're a lot more flexible, and so am I."

How was it different? Before, I asked Ava frantically, "How am I supposed to juggle all of this?" Now, I had perspective, "Before, the juggling was with an end in sight. There was an end date. Before, it was about launching. Now it's about continual growth and maturity. Now I am juggling things that are ongoing. They won't go away. It's a permanent responsibility. It needs to be part of who I am."

"Don't worry", Ava said. "It's definitely part of who you are. I see it."

Most of the skills learned in preparing for launch were not transitory after all. The need didn't go away after the launch milestone was achieved. So, while this new 'world' of practical things seemed new, it was important to keep doing those things. Practical matters needed to be embraced, and not despised. They were not in the way or 'unspiritual'. They were part of being effective spiritually. Prayer, conviction, sacrifice and anointing could not be replaced. However, planning, management, delegation, calendars, schedules, financial and fiscal management, progress reviews, plan adjustments, community involvement and relations, and communication plans would still be needed also.

I had a long list before that I recited to Ava. I had a new

The Juggler - Reprise

list of ongoing activities to juggle. "Well, for starters, ongoing church operations and administration, board meetings, business meetings, weekly services, teaching plans, websites, social media, outreach, and leadership development are part of those ongoing things that cannot be neglected."

"It's good I learned to be calmer", I said with a faint smile. "I hope that holds true. For this second act, there's more to juggle. There will be new things. The transition to a permanent facility, building improvements and remodels, purchase and replacement of sound and audio equipment, the development and maintenance of facilities, parking lots, bathrooms, classrooms, office and Sunday School supplies, staff and payroll are just some of the new things to manage. Starting to sound familiar? This list seems as endless and daunting as the first." Ava said, "A very wise man once told me about things being 'fitly framed'. I suggest you find that man and talk to him." She wrapped those comforting arms around me, and said, "I love you, Edwin. I believe in you."

The practical importance of delegation was still essential. It wasn't a mystery. For each activity and responsibility, I had to decide what to delegate, how much to delegate, what the levels of authority and accountability would be, and what items I should retain. Trust was the challenge, but it wasn't complicated. To be as effective as possible, I had to delegate as much as I could.

Planning was more important than ever. This adage was still true: "If you fail to plan, you plan to fail." Now an advocate of planning, I put these words into a lesson, "Planning is an essential investment. It will ultimately save time and money. As responsible agents, our natures say we must act. As wise agents, we know that before doing, we

The Juggler - Reprise

must plan. As the responsibilities mount, planning brings calmness. It is the catalyst of success. The alternative is chaos."

"Well said", she replied.

READING GUIDE POINTS:
1. Church planters' prayers are tangible and specific. Learning is an intangible that is seldom the focus of our prayers.
2. What you have learned to this point is one of the strongest and most important benefits
3. Learning is the substance of growth
4. What you have learned will not be forgotten
5. You have learned that you can trust the Lord and faithful, Spirit-filled people
6. You have learned that the Word of God is powerful
7. You have learned the importance of balancing the spiritual and the practical
8. You have learned not to panic
9. You have learned to be flexible
10. You have learned the importance of planning and delegation
11. What you have learned to this point has prepared you to juggle even more responsibility moving forward

The Juggler - Reprise

> **References from:**
> ***Effective Christianity: Managing Life's Projects***
> - Chapter 5, page 50
>   - Be honest with results. Don't ignore what the data is telling you.
>   - We often focus on bad news. There is good news as well. Report both.
> - Chapter 6, page 58
>   - Effective listening is coupled with response
> - Chapter 6, page 59
>   - Spiritual people must be effective, and an effective life demands action
> - Chapter 6, page 60
>   - Spiritual fulfillment is not found by accident. The fulfillment we all seek requires response. Faith is coupled with action.
> - Chapter 8, page 80
>   - Nearly every project is complicated and requires skillful balancing of conflicting goals and priorities
> - Chapter 10, page 96
>   - Faith does not ignore risk. It prepares us for the risks in our journey.

Everything

During this tremendous journey and looking back on this inexplicably fulfilling result, I was reminded of a conversation. I was having lunch one day with one of the strongest supporters of our young church that was only beginning. He was very supportive, and a prayerful man that prayed for us and the church. He would always do everything he could do to help. He was one of those blessings that a pastor needed. He would always try to encourage me. He understood and appreciated what I was doing as the pastor. Not everyone had that understanding. Just having someone who showed appreciation was so important.

There was some measure of trust that developed. Without betraying confidence, I was able, at times, to carefully explain how challenging it could be sometimes to be a pastor and to plant a church. Usually, he would listen, and in his listening encourage.

On a particular day, I will say it was noteworthy, the conversation was a bit different. I had expressed, in some way, a challenge I had faced. Then, with no disrespect and an earned and perhaps God-directed openness, he said:

> "You know, pastor, you're not the only one who has to deal with challenges in their work."

I was accustomed to challenging others in their pity, but I was humbly on the receiving end this time.

He described a story that happened early in his career doing engineering work:

> "I had only been out of college for a few years. I was given an important assignment to review facility requirements, compliance with requirements, shortfalls and

recommendations. The assignment was not given directly by my boss, but by the division manager. I took the assignment seriously, was honored that I had been asked to do it, and studied carefully all of the requirements that applied to that facility. It took some time to review, analyze and document everything. I did my very best to prepare a convincing report. I scheduled a meeting with my boss and the division manager to report my findings. I went through my presentations, and when finished, I hoped and expected agreement and endorsement of corrective measures I had recommended.

The response was a bit surprising. The division manager began asking questions. He asked many questions. There were important matters that he felt should also have been addressed. He disagreed with some of the recommended solutions and their wisdom. He questioned the cost and the timeframe of the solutions. He didn't really agree with the overall approach taken. Thankfully, he wasn't angry or upset. He said to take these thoughts and suggestions and start over.

It was a devasting blow to my ego. It could have been devastating to my career had the division manager reacted as you would expect. I asked myself, 'How could I have missed the mark so badly?'

A valuable lesson was learned. During all of the study, review, analysis, and development of recommendations, there had been no ongoing discussion or review with the division manager. I had taken the assignment with joy, worked diligently on my own to do the task, and come back when I was finished. The simple lesson was that the more important the assignment, the more important it is to keep key stakeholders involved during the process. The worst thing

Everything

you can do is to wait until the end to find out that you completely missed what the customer was expecting. It's important to take the time to keep the right people informed during the course of your work.

The effort eventually was successful, meeting the division manager's expectations. But it was a difficult and somewhat painful and embarrassing learning experience. During feedback, I told the divisions manager how difficult the job had been. The division manager smiled, and somewhat smugly said:

> 'If the job was easy, we wouldn't have given it to you.'"

I could only grin and nod my head to my supportive friend to convey that the point had been made well.

Sometimes, I felt like that was spoken to me. Honestly, this wasn't easy. Planting a church was extremely challenging. It seemed, at times, and perhaps often, that it was the hardest thing in the world to do. In weak but understandable moments, I would feel that the Lord had only called me to do hard things.

> "Why am I the one called to do such a hard thing? Why weren't others called to things this hard?"

In the telling of all of these stories, it was important not to leave the wrong impression. The intent was, or course, to be positive, and to highlight things that were helpful. It could have appeared, though, that with proper planning, management and administration, all problems and struggles could have been prevented. The message might have been that it was possible to plant a church without challenge or problems. That, simply, was not the message. These stories

Everything

were told to help others in their struggles, but they were not told to suggest that struggle could be avoided. It would have been very wrong to suggest that planning would eliminate struggle, or to conclude that your journey should be one of ease.

The true message was this. Planning prepared for the problems and issues, and helped me get through them. It did not prevent them.

I didn't want anyone to be misled. God hadn't called me to comfort, a casual commitment, or convenience. He had called me to consecration, devotion and sacrifice. He even told me to expect persecution for His name. Living for Him wasn't easy. He never said it would be. Jesus was my supreme example of complete commitment and sacrifice. He had called me to follow His example. It wasn't easy for Him to fulfill His divine purpose. It wouldn't be easy for me either.

Along with all of the positive approaches and helpful advice, this was still true, and I had to make it clear:

"It will take everything."

Everything had to be laid on the altar for His will. It would still require sacrifice and enduring challenges. I had talked with many others who had been on this journey. Everyone's story was not identical, but sacrifice was never absent from the story. Most had times when they had to cut back on clothes, vacations, food and restaurants. For many, every member of the family was working to help pay the family's personal bills and then to cover church expenses as well. Small churches had little financial flexibility. New converts had no experience in tithing or sacrificial giving. With even the best management, there would be times when

Everything

there wasn't enough money. Careers and professional ambition would have to be sacrificed. The nearly universal element in their stories was they had to save money any way they could.

As great as the financial strain would be, it would take more than money. There would be little to no spare time. Spending quality time with children and spouses would be difficult, and easily they would feel neglected. They would deserve respect, devotion and an appreciation that was impossible to express. As determined and intentional as any might be, it would be challenging to force the time with them that they deserved.

Integrity demanded that I make the required devotion and sacrifice, and the difficulties clear. But to stop there would have been wrong also. For in spite of the challenges, there would yet be a strong and positive result.

I had spoken with others who were on the journey of planting a church. I knew of their struggle, their commitment, and their sacrifice. I knew of their joys and successes as well. I knew there were moments when their calling might be in question. Discouragement still would come. Faith would still be required. To these new, brave warriors I would say, "You can do it. There are things that will help you get through the challenges, but the challenges will still come. They are a necessary part of your calling. Yes, be prepared. Know that, in spite of your best efforts, there will be struggle. But don't prepare for disappointment and failure. Prepare for a reward that's more meaningful because of the challenges you endured. Start and continue your patient journey with your eyes open. Fight. Endure. Take advantage of every help you have. Learn from the wisdom of everyone who has gone before you. Finish."

Not every lesson learned was about failure or mistake. There were so many positive lessons. One of the most important lessons was what I learned about my children, Daniel and Mia. Certainly, this journey shaped their lives. But they surprised and amazed me. I had moments fearing that they might be bitter. To the contrary, they inspired me. They were devoted and willing to do their part. That devotion and sacrifice became part of who they were. It endured in them, and I was so proud of what they became through it. Looking back revealed another positive message. We could look back, and know that we did everything we could. We held nothing back.

"You know, pastor, you're not the only one who has to deal with challenges in their work." Those words stuck with me. I wasn't the only one who dealt with challenge. The truth was that every calling was challenging, important, and hard. Every calling took determination and sacrifice. I could feel sorry for myself, and think no one had it as hard as me. That thinking was short-sighted and self-centered. Other people sacrificed as much as I did. Being in the ministry didn't justify self-pity. Ministers weren't the only ones who dealt with struggle. Everyone who devoted their life to Jesus had to endure by faith. There were people in other parts of the world who lived at a standard of living much lower than me. Yet they were joyous and willing to risk their lives for the Gospel.

So, I prayed:

"Lord, open my eyes. Help me to keep looking on others. If I can only see more clearly, and if I can only see as you want me to see, I won't complain as much. I won't pity

Everything

myself as much. Lord, you didn't call me to pity and complaint. You called me to a great thing. It is an honor to be asked to plant a church. I am honored that you have such confidence in me. This is a noble calling. Nothing is more valuable or more fulfilling that seeing Your will accomplished. Nothing is more rewarding for me than to see this will accomplished."

Everything had to be laid on the alter to plant a church. And when everything was required, there were two things that I found were certain. The first certainty was that I had to be absolutely certain of my calling if I was to endure. The struggle would be too much without the certain foundation of that calling. But with a certain calling, it would be more than a struggle. Through the struggle, there would be joy, and overwhelming satisfaction of seeing a great eternal result. The second certainty was that I would never regret any of the sacrifice. It was, in fact, that complete commitment that brought the greatest satisfaction. If I had held back, I may have questioned whether I had done enough, and regretted my lack of commitment. But I had no such regret. I knew I had done all that I could. I knew I had held nothing back.

Everything

READING GUIDE POINTS:
1. Yes, planting a church is extremely challenging, but you're not the only one who has to deal with challenges in their work and life
2. Planning prepares you for problems and issues, and helps get you through them. It does not prevent them.
3. God doesn't call you to comfort, casual commitment, or convenience. He calls you to consecration, devotion and sacrifice.
4. You still have to lay everything on the altar for His will
5. You must devote all of your time and finances to His will
6. Giving priority to your family will be challenging
7. Your example and message to others is that they too can do this
8. Hold nothing back
9. If you hold nothing back, you will not regret any sacrifice

Everything

References from:
Effective Christianity: Managing Life's Projects

- Chapter 1, page 10
  - Struggle tests vision and commitment
- Chapter 1, page 11
  - True success is coupled with sacrifice. It does not take from others; it sacrifices for their benefit.
- Chapter 3, page 39
  - Love is an unfailing commitment to sacrifice and selflessness
- Chapter 6, page 85
  - Living in the Spirit is not easy. Focus and commitment are required in the face of distraction, criticism and temptation.
- Chapter 6, page 90
  - Perseverance is more than unresponsive stubbornness; it is an unfailing commitment that is continually responsive to His leading.
- Chapter 9, page 135
  - Growth requires commitment. Gifts of those who are effective are coupled with maturity and wisdom. Through experience, they become more effective.
- Chapter 10, page 143
  - You must risk everything to be a disciple of Jesus
- Chapter 10, page 149
  - Dreams are not achieved easily, and challenges will arise. Do not assume:
    - Everything will always go well
    - Everyone will support you
    - You know how to plan your own future

A Legacy of Service

> *A son's (and daughter's) perspective(s):*
>
> I am Daniel, the son of church planters. You have heard their stories of the journey to plant a church. My sister, Mia, and I talked to our parents. We told them that the story(ies) they tell could not be complete without our perspective as their children. We asked if we could add one more dimension to the story.
>
> Truly, it is a family that is called to plant a church. As it is for all children, parents make decisions, hopefully with the leading of the Lord, that change their children's lives as well. In that sense, we too were called to this city.
>
> Though I will tell the story, this is a joint narrative from me and my sister. The story, though, is not just our own. Mia and I saw much, but there was more. We knew of the experiences of other children who were called, with their parents, to other cities. That broader view is also important. It should be told as well.
>
> We will do our best to tell you two things. First, we will tell you what we experienced. This includes what we experienced as children, but mostly, what we observed in our parents. Second, we will tell you how this journey affected and shaped our lives. There is much to say.

We were normal children, wanting normal things. Playing, having friends, creating memories with family (especially cousins our age) were just a few of the normal things we desired.

Our childhood wasn't always as normal as we hoped. Ignorant and, at times, unconcerned with the plight of others,

A Legacy of Service

we thought we were alone in that oddity. I told Mia, "Surely, no one experienced things as weird as we did." Truthfully though, we weren't alone. We've since found out that other children had reasons that their childhood wasn't normal. Their lives were interesting too, or course. But our experiences and the reason for them were unique to our story. Our reason was that our family was planting a church. Few have experienced these things.

Christmas was one of those things we wanted to be normal. We were always excited as Christmas approached. I remember telling my mom, "I like presents, being with family, eating good food, especially dessert, and that everyone will be happy." Yes, we knew it was all about Jesus and His birth. We heard and understood the 'real meaning of Christmas'. Yet, as children, the wonder and excitement still captivated us. There was a feeling that we cherished. We didn't want it to go away.

One particular Christmas exemplified well why even Christmas wouldn't always be normal. Our special Christmas service at church was over. We were on break from school. The extra time only heightened our excitement. I got up on Christmas Eve and said to Mia, "Tomorrow it will finally be here. Tomorrow is Christmas!" But first, dad said, "We are going to another city nearby."

Another family was planting a church near us. We knew them well. Though it wasn't easy for us, their financial struggle seemed to be worse. I hadn't paid much attention to it, but mom and dad had. Dad told us, "Their financial situation is bad enough that the children qualify for free lunches and books at school. It isn't well-known. They are a bit embarrassed. So please don't say anything. They want to

A Legacy of Service

help others, rather than ask for help. More importantly, they don't want others to worry about them." But mom and dad did know. Mom said, with no resistance from dad, "We can't do nothing." We helped mom wrap some presents for them while dad went and bought groceries. When he returned, we got in the car, and drove to their home. With tears in her eyes, mom gave these great people what we had, and said, "We just wanted to do what we could to help." As we left, Mia and I were glad for our friends, but also touched by the determined generosity of our parents.

Truthfully, this was not a rare event. As Mia has said so often, "Mom and dad were always giving to people in need. Somehow, even if we were having our own troubles, mom and dad would sacrifice. There was no hesitation to giving. The needs of others always came first. We learned to expect it."

But now we could put that aside. It was Christmas Eve. We were headed home. We had done our good deed and helped someone. Now we would enjoy our time together. Or so we thought.

There was a wonderful man in our church who had no family or close friends. Christmas wasn't a busy time for him. Often, he spent Christmas alone. He loved mom and dad. He knew, as did so many, that they cared. In my excitement, I would forget. But nearly every Christmas Eve, this man would knock at the door. Dad would open the door, and without hesitation say, "Please come in." Mom would smile, and with a tone of welcome and excitement, invite him, "Please stay for a while." Mia and I would look at each other, roll our eyes, and softly say to each other, "Here we go again". At the time, we didn't appreciate the intrusion. Now we look back, and

A Legacy of Service

realize it was yet another manifestation of lives devoted to serving others. The fellowship and warmth, no doubt, assisted this lonely man in his walk with the Lord. The church did care. He wasn't alone. Invariably, by the time he left, dad would say, "Well, it's too late open presents now", and we had to quell our excitement until Christmas morning.

As an old song said, 'It will be hard to sleep tonight'. Somehow, we got there. It was Christmas morning. In near perfect unison, Mia and I would say, "No mom, we don't care about breakfast. We want to open presents." With complete confidence, and what seemed to be no sympathy, she said, "We will not open any presents until we've had breakfast and thanked the Lord for His blessings." Then dad said, "Besides, we will read the Christmas story together as well." "OK", we both said, with a big sigh.

We did have breakfast, we did read the Christmas story, and we did, finally, open presents. I don't actually remember what our presents were that particular Christmas. There was something else that was more important. After we opened our presents with great joy, at the same moment, Mia and I then realized mom and dad had no presents. We asked them, "Where are your presents?" "Oh, it's OK", mom said. "We don't need anything." They had spent what little money they had for each other on the presents and groceries for the other family that was struggling more. We were shocked, but only momentarily. Then, as children, we were able to accept this and revive our own excitement. But something happened. We may have forgotten at that moment, but the image and the example would stick with us still today.

It might seem that this was an unusual story. No, it

A Legacy of Service

wasn't unusual at all. This was what our lives were like. Church wasn't something we did; it was our life. The whole family was involved. We were all devoted to the work of the Lord. Each of us were consumed with the pursuit of establishing a church in this city. Maybe it was even an obsession. People had to be saved. Even though we were children, Mia and I would go with mom and dad when they counseled people. We saw how they provided comfort and prayed with anyone who needed help.

    It took every moment of all our lives. But there was no complaint and no bitterness. Mom and dad never said anything bad about anybody, even though we knew there was good reason to do so. They just weren't those kinds of people. If there was anything good about someone, they shared it freely. Otherwise, they kept it to themselves. Like the family that we helped on Christmas, they didn't want others to worry about them and their needs. They never sought attention or recognition. Service was all that mattered. As their children, that determination to serve became part of who we were. Mia and I couldn't imagine living any other way.

    We had great admiration for our parents. We saw their devotion and commitment. Dad would work hard on his job. He was always studying his Bible. There were so many duties as a pastor that only we saw. Yet, like the man who would come on Christmas Eve, he always made time for people. Mom was no different. She was always trying to do more. Her creativity was inspiring. She would do something to add a special touch to everything. Still today, Mia will say, "Daniel, this is how mom would do it. we've got to do something extra." I always knew what would come next, "Come on,

A Legacy of Service

Daniel. You're going to help." As it was with mom, I could not argue with helping.

We saw two great examples of strong, unshakeable faith. Dad seemed so strong. No obstacle would stop him. Mom's hope never faded. When troubles would come, she would say, "It's another opportunity for God to do a miracle."

We understood what it was to have a burden for the lost. People were being saved, and that truly was all that mattered. Dad would remind us when our reward would come, "There will be an eternal reward. Our recognition will come in heaven, when we see the faces of all those that were saved because of what we did. Then, as it is now, it will be worth every sacrifice". We knew those words were true, and there was coming a great reward for the sacrifice of our parents.

Honestly, it was not only a life of service. It was a life of sacrifice as well. Sometimes we went without so we could take care of the church. We cut back on personal conveniences, clothes, vacations, food and restaurants. Every spare dollar was devoted to the church. All that mattered was the work of God.

Yes, there were times when it seemed the commitment to the church was so strong that our family was neglected. As children, we felt at times that we were neglected, especially when mom and dad had so much time for others, and we wanted more of their time as well. Then there were times when everything else was set aside, and we would go somewhere as a family. Those times were special.

My father was so devoted, he would put his life at risk. Late one night, or maybe it was very early one morning, there was a phone call. This wasn't unusual. Late night calls for

A Legacy of Service

prayer were common. There was muted conversation, and dad got dressed hurriedly. This time mom didn't go. We found out why later. The call was from a couple in our church whose son had barricaded himself in their bathroom with a gun. Instead of calling the police, they called their pastor. Dad arrived, and eventually convinced the man to come out. But not before he had shot a hole in the floor of the bathroom. Once we heard the details, we were terrified. That night would never be forgotten.

There were stories of generosity from others as well. There is one episode that will always remind me that others were willing to sacrifice too. We were at a point where things were financially difficult. We were cutting back on all of those things I mentioned earlier. While in that struggle, we got the terrible news that our grandfather had passed away. It was my dad's father. We knew he had been sick. We thought he would get better. Our dad had said, "He always bounces back." This time, he didn't bounce back. Dad told mom, "Honey, there's just not enough money for me to go to the funeral." Somehow, word got out that dad couldn't go. A man in the church came to the house, and said, "Pastor, is it true your father passed away, and that you can't afford to go to his funeral?" Dad replied, "Well, things are a little tight right now. I should probably stay here." The man, said, "No, you need to be with your family", and handed dad the money so he could go. Mom said what she had said so many times before, "The Lord always provides." These testimonies were also part of what we remembered.

Despite the sacrifice, our bond as a family was strong. Through times of disappointment, it was always clear that our parents loved us. The spiritual connection we shared was a strong pillar in our lives. My father baptized me. He baptized Mia. There were nights, before I received the Holy Ghost, that I would tell my parents, "I'm afraid that the Lord will come. I know I'm not ready yet." In the middle of the night, they prayed with me. I didn't need a crowd. When it was just the three (or four) of us, we could still feel his presence as we prayed. They were praying with me when I received the Holy Ghost.

We could talk to our parents about anything. One time, Mia had a few friends at church that were getting into things that weren't right. They would stop talking when she approached. She told us, "I feel so lonely when they do that." Dad explained, "Friendship isn't only about what you need from your friends. It's more important that you give something to them."

There was a bond with other children who were like us. We learned that they too had stories, and we realized that we didn't have things so bad after all.

One family's church was located in their home. Naturally, everything went to help the church. There was a wonderful lady in the church who led the Sunday School. For a Sunday School contest, the lady asked, "What should the prizes be for the Sunday School contest?" The pastor's daughter answered, "A candy bar." The other children looked at her curiously, and said, "No, we want Cabbage Patch dolls." For the other children, a candy bar wasn't special. They had those all of the time. But the pastor's daughter rarely had a candy bar. To her, just a candy bar was special.

Another family left the financial security of two jobs to go where they had no jobs, no home and no school. They took on the responsibility of a church with no church income.

A Legacy of Service

They were forced to live in the basement of a neighboring church. They finally found jobs paying much less than they had made before, but they had to do whatever was necessary. To support the church, they had two mortgages, in addition to their family personal expenses. Every member of the family was working to support the church and get by. Like us, everything was devoted to the church. One day, at the grocery store, the daughter asked for a special kind of cereal. The mother said, "I'm sorry, we can't afford that." She told us, "It seemed like such a simple thing." She began crying, asking, "Why are we so poor?"

For some, it wasn't only about their struggle. There were stories of the struggles of others, including their own parents. One daughter said there were always children in trouble around them whose lives were at risk. More than once, they would keep children in their home until a safer option was found. Another daughter said the most difficult part was seeing her parents' struggle. When they weren't treated right, she wanted desperately to do anything to help them. One day, after she felt her father had been mistreated, she yelled, "If you do this again, I'll kill you." We understood her desperation.

To some, these stories seem amazing or even depressing. They might evoke pity. "Surely", some would say, "you must be bitter". To the contrary, and strongly, we say, "No. We aren't bitter. We don't begrudge the sacrifice. Mia and I cherish what we saw, and what we experienced. We cherish the example we saw. We would do the same thing now. As it was when we were children, our lives now are about service to others. We never questioned that we should do our part. We wanted to help as much as we could. None of

A Legacy of Service

that has changed. What we went through made us what we are. We are happy. We are blessed. We have no regrets."

READING GUIDE POINTS:
1. Your children are also called to help plant this church
2. What your children experience will change their lives too
3. The legacy your children will see is one of giving, sacrifice and service to others
4. Church isn't just something you do; it is your life
5. Your children will admire you
6. You are examples of strong, unshakeable faith
7. Your children will learn of the sacrifice of others
8. Your children will see and have compassion for the struggles of others
9. As it is for you, your children will not regret their calling or service

References from:
Effective Christianity: Managing Life's Projects
- Chapter 1, page 8
  - Success does not free you from service. To the contrary, success provides greater opportunity to help others. Take advantage of that opportunity.
  - True success is coupled with sacrifice. It does not take from others; it sacrifices for their benefit.
- Chapter 3, page 25
  - Love is an unfailing commitment to sacrifice and selflessness

A Vision for Reproduction

There was a lot of farm land surrounding our city. I asked a member of the Chamber of Commerce to tell me how the city developed. "This area developed like typical farming communities. Originally, businesses concentrated in a central location to serve the needs of farmers. Later, businesses diversified, and the city diversified as well. People are drawn here for many reasons now. Growth, expansion and diversity are part of this community's foresight, which we do our best to promote. But the city is rooted in agriculture, and a strong farming community helps define our heritage and culture."

Talking to farmers was a regular occurrence if that opportunity was taken. Many didn't seize the moment, but I had learned its importance. It was often simple conversation, always honest, and quite refreshing. To those who genuinely appreciated what farmers did, that appreciation was perceived, and there was a welcoming friendship that awaited. I enjoyed the exchange; I looked forward to it. I learned much.

Apparently, my appreciation was seen, and to my benefit, rewarded. For on some occasions, my new farmer friends would say, "Come on out and visit any time you want. We'd be happy to see you." I welcomed and responded to the invitation many times.

The open grandeur of the fields inspired me. There was a quiet, almost solemn beauty in a simplicity which we all unknowingly sought. The most important activity was the silent, steady development of the crop. When my life seemed so complicated, I longed to go to such a place. It refreshed my soul, and restored my spirit as God's creation was divinely designed to do. Basics were not an aside; they were the core of this kind of life.

Farmers knew about planting and nurturing. They knew about harvest. Planting and cultivating were absolutely essential. But they are to an end. During one of my visits, this friend discussed his intention, "The focus is the harvest. The quiet days, the perils of flood and drought, the pestilence of creatures of all kinds, these things are all part of the only thing that matters. The work is hard and the risks are real. The field may be beautiful. But, 'Is there a harvest?', is the only question."

With few exceptions, there were two primary crops in our area, winter wheat and corn. Their seasons differed. Through this, the Lord had taught me an important lesson about reproduction. It changed me profoundly. While devoted singularly to our planting, we hadn't valued or even considered that there was another crop. Though we focused on our own harvest, it was not the only one. There was more than one field. It was His intention that all be harvested. One crop was not enough.

Farmers knew the planting seasons well. Their story was a matter of fact, "Winter wheat is planted in late fall. October is the usual start around here. Waiting in cold soil throughout the winter, winter wheat is ready as soon as the soil begins to warm, and bursts forth early in the spring. It's an early harvest. Winter wheat is harvested in June."

That was phase one. Corn was a different cycle. "It's not planted until May. It doesn't have a winter cycle. Rather than being in the cold soil, ready as soon as the early warmth of spring begins, corn is planted later. As winter wheat is nearing harvest, the cycle for corn is just beginning. It is

A Vision for Reproduction

nearly the end of spring before it's launched. Unlike the winter wheat, which survives the cold winter, and is harvested before summer arrives, corn must survive the heat and the struggle of the summer months. In fact, it's the heat that fuels it's abundance. Long after the winter wheat has been harvested, corn is still growing. The time to nurture is later. It is harvested in fall. September is the time to reap corn."

There were so many simple, yet important lessons to be learned about harvesting. These lessons gave me profound insight into another personal responsibility. It was about the responsibility to reproduce. But the responsibility to reproduce was more than personal. It needed to be borne by our church.

I felt that the Lord had given me a message to proclaim. This new burden burned in me. It had to be expressed. Soon I would preach about these four lessons. I wrote them down.

1. **"The first lesson is that there is more than one harvest.** With each season, there is a new harvest. There is a new field to plant, other soil to be nurtured, and another harvest to be reaped."
2. **"The second lesson is that each harvest is different.** Each crop is different. It is that difference that gives us opportunity. Rather than an impossible task of harvesting every crop at once, there is an appointed time to move from one harvest to another. When one harvest is secured, it's time to add another crop to the storehouse."
3. **"The third lesson is that each harvest is important.** We cannot survive on one crop. Weakness, malnutrition and

A Vision for Reproduction

disease will be the result. It is the blend of these many harvests that gives us strength."

4. **"The fourth lesson is that harvesting is ongoing.** One harvest leads to another. We need each one. There is a short time of rest, but it is only that – short. It is a time for refreshing and renewal. The cycles may differ. But one thing is the same. When each cycle is complete, it repeats. As long as the cycle repeats, there is a harvest to be reaped."

   I had been so passionate about this city. That passion was all consuming. The Lord was dealing with me. It was time for an even bigger vision. I felt He was saying, "There is more than one harvest. There is more than one city that needs to be reached. Each harvest is different. How each city will be reached will be different. Each harvest is important. In My divine plan, each city is as important as your city. Someone needs the same passion for other cities. The harvest is ongoing. You can never stop reaching. The harvest isn't complete."

   Our church was blessed. As God had willed, a church had been planted in this city. By His grace, it was becoming a strong church. But there was yet more. He was calling again. He was calling our entire church.

   I did preach that message. In concluding, I exhorted this great people, "What He has done for us must be reproduced in others. As Antioch and Ephesus were centers of reproduction, we too must reproduce. The harvest is not complete. There are other cities that must be reached. It is His will that all come to salvation, and know the abiding joy of His presence. They need the Word, they need the Holy Ghost, they need the eternal, transcendent hope that can only come

A Vision for Reproduction

from a life devoted to His service."

I encouraged them to look ahead, "We look beyond what is. There is a blessed future that can be another part of our collective legacy. We will reach beyond our city. God is calling us to be ready even now. He has given us a vision for reproduction. That vision will be, no, it must now be, part of our culture. There are churches to plant. We will send them to that new harvest. It is a harvest that He has ordained."

Our people responded. Their eyes were opened to the harvest. I could sense their burden. They told me, "We were moved, and we want to be part of a bigger harvest." A vision was dawning. I couldn't be satisfied with simply preaching about it. I didn't want them to be complacent. I couldn't be either. As always, action was required.

There were two fundamental components to vision. Those two components were exposure and communication.

When anyone in our church said, "We feel a burden", I urged them, "Go, visit unchurched cities and pray for them". I could not hold them back. I had been there. I knew that if they did go, that exposure would plant a seed of awareness. A passion to meet the need of the lost would be incited. When that passion ignited, as I prayed it would, I had already determined I would say, "I encourage that passion. I will fan the flame. That call will grow louder. A burden will overtake your heart. You must respond."

That is the vision we would communicate to our church. Consistent communication solidified vision. It fueled determination. It brought results.

My vision was beyond us in another capacity. I would cast a vision for reproduction beyond our city limits. Yes, I would encourage church planters from among us. But they

A Vision for Reproduction

didn't have to be from us to have my support. I would encourage church planters no matter where they were. What was important was that they were called, and they had answered the call. I would say to them, "My own journey, this sometimes frightening, yet joyous journey, joins my heart with your burden."

With this fresh vision for reproduction in mind, I prayed to the Lord, "When people from our church are called to go, I will not hold them back. I will give them to the harvest. I will go with them. When others are called, I will do my very best to support and encourage. It's now my turn. It's my time to stand for the furtherance of the Gospel to others. I will be an example. I will give. I will go and help. When they need help and a voice of encouragement, I will mentor those who have taken this daunting, but noble, divine calling."

To you called to the harvest, and to you who will support those who accept that call, I encourage you, "Listen. Respond. Join in the work of the Kingdom. His Word must be proclaimed. His Spirit must be known. His will must be done, IN ALL THE EARTH! OH, PRAISE THE GLORIOUS NAME OF JESUS! HE IS WORTHY!"

READING GUIDE POINTS:
1. The focus is the harvest
2. There is more than one harvest
3. Each harvest is different
4. Each harvest is important
5. Harvesting is ongoing
6. The two fundamental components to vision are exposure and communication

A Vision for Reproduction

> **References from:**
> ***Effective Christianity: Managing Life's Projects***
> - Chapter 1, page 5
>   - Our plans, our actions, and effectiveness are all judged by whether we reached the world with the message of Christ. Everything is measured against the mandate to fulfill the Great Commission.
> - Chapter 1, page 6
>   - We identify with Jesus Christ alone, pledge our lives to Him in repentance, and identify with Him in baptism. It is His Spirit that reigns in our souls. It is His name that saves.
> - Case study, The Apostles, page 113
>   - The approach taken by the Apostoles was:
>   - To choose and develop strong, passionate leaders
>   - To identify strategic locations for outreach
>   - To pursue individual direction with anointing
>   - To develop a strong, sustaining team
> - Case study, The Apostles, page 114
>   - It is His ultimate purpose that every man have His redemptive hope

APPENDIX 1
Church Planter Scorecard

The Church Planter Scorecard consists of six individual scorecards:

1. Spiritual Practical Balance
2. Scope Management
3. Schedule Management
4. Resource Management
5. Risk Management
6. Spiritual Priorities

These topics follow the narratives in this book, as well as topics from the referenced text, *Effective Christianity: Managing Life's Projects*. Each topic is assessed independently. Summary results are tabulated. Then you will identify area(s) for improvement, and steps for improvement.

You may want to make copies for later use by some of your teams, team members, etc.

Spiritual Practical Balance Scorecard

1. I am certain of my calling to plant a church in this city.

   Not   Absolutely
   sure   certain

   1 --- 2 --- 3 --- 4 --- 5

2. I am committed to Apostolic doctrine and practice.

   Time to   Fully
   change   committed

   1 --- 2 --- 3 --- 4 --- 5

3. I am steadfast in my personal devotions.

   No   Daily
   devotions   devotions

   1 --- 2 --- 3 --- 4 --- 5

4. I expect challenges that must be endured, managed and overcome.

   Won't be   I will
   difficult   endure

   1 --- 2 --- 3 --- 4 --- 5

5. I believe in the value of practical skills for the church.

   Only "spiritual"   Practical is
   things   essential

   1 --- 2 --- 3 --- 4 --- 5

6. I have documented a long-term plan for this church.

   No   Documented
   plan   plan

   1 --- 2 --- 3 --- 4 --- 5

7. Spiritual fulfillment demands that I act when the Lord speaks to me.

   Wait for   Response
   god to act   requires action

   1 --- 2 --- 3 --- 4 --- 5

8. I have personal goals.

   No   Personal
   goals   goals set

   1 --- 2 --- 3 --- 4 --- 5

9. Goals have been set for our church.

   No   Church
   goals   goals set

   1 --- 2 --- 3 --- 4 --- 5

10. I believe effective planning is needed to fulfill God's will for this church.

    No   Planning is
    planning   essential

    1 --- 2 --- 3 --- 4 --- 5

TOTAL _____

Scope Management Scorecard

1. For each of our church's plans, the end product is clearly defined.

   No   Well
   plans   defined
   1 --- 2 --- 3 --- 4 --- 5

2. Our goals and end products are communicated transparently.

   No   Communicated
   communication   openly
   1 --- 2 --- 3 --- 4 --- 5

3. The tasks for our projects are defined and documented.

   No   Documented
   tasks   well
   1 --- 2 --- 3 --- 4 --- 5

4. We estimate the cost for each church project.

   No   Every
   estimates   project
   1 --- 2 --- 3 --- 4 --- 5

5. We control our projects to only the tasks needed for that project.

   No   Well
   control   controlled
   1 --- 2 --- 3 --- 4 --- 5

6. The money designated for a project is spent only on that project.

   No   Well
   control   controlled
   1 --- 2 --- 3 --- 4 --- 5

7. We track what a project costs compared to that project's estimate.

   No   Good
   tracking   tracking
   1 --- 2 --- 3 --- 4 --- 5

8. We objectively analyze why costs deviate from what was estimated.

   No   Disciplined
   analysis   analysis
   1 --- 2 --- 3 --- 4 --- 5

9. We take corrective action to control deviation in project cost.

   No   Disciplined
   corrections   corrections
   1 --- 2 --- 3 --- 4 --- 5

10. We openly communicate how well we control our costs.

    No   Open
    communication   communication
    1 --- 2 --- 3 --- 4 --- 5

TOTAL _____

Schedule Management Scorecard

1. All of our church projects are managed through a master schedule.

       No   Every
   schedules   project
   1 --- 2 --- 3 --- 4 --- 5

2. Each project is broken down into specific tasks needed for the project.

       No   Detailed
    tasks   tasks
   1 --- 2 --- 3 --- 4 --- 5

3. Each project's tasks are sequenced in a schedule.

       No   Completely
   sequencing   sequenced
   1 --- 2 --- 3 --- 4 --- 5

4. Resources are identified for each project task.

     None   All
   identified   identified
   1 --- 2 --- 3 --- 4 --- 5

5. Cost and duration are estimated for each project task.

       No   Detailed
   estimates   estimates
   1 --- 2 --- 3 --- 4 --- 5

6. We control our projects to only the tasks needed for that project.

       No   Well
    control   controlled
   1 --- 2 --- 3 --- 4 --- 5

7. We track project completions compared to their estimated completions.

       No   Good
   tracking   tracking
   1 --- 2 --- 3 --- 4 --- 5

8. We objectively analyze why completions deviate from their estimates.

       No   Disciplined
   analysis   analysis
   1 --- 2 --- 3 --- 4 --- 5

9. We take corrective action to control deviation in project completions.

       No   Disciplined
   corrections   corrections
   1 --- 2 --- 3 --- 4 --- 5

10. We openly communicate how well we control our schedules.

         No   Open
    communication   communication
    1 --- 2 --- 3 --- 4 --- 5

    TOTAL _____

Resource Management Scorecard

1. Our summary team plan defines the purpose of every church team.
           No   Purpose
           plan   defined
          1 --- 2 --- 3 --- 4 --- 5

2. The qualities for each team's members are defined.
           No   Qualities
       definition   defined
          1 --- 2 --- 3 --- 4 --- 5

3. We will follow the Lord in determining who is qualified.
      Pre-defined   Spiritually
        criteria   sensitive
          1 --- 2 --- 3 --- 4 --- 5

4. We have a staffing plan to identify good fit for each team member.
           No   Complete
          plan   plan
          1 --- 2 --- 3 --- 4 --- 5

5. Resources are identified for each church project.
           Not   Resources
        tracked   identified
          1 --- 2 --- 3 --- 4 --- 5

6. Spiritual development and fulfillment of all team members is important.
           Not   Key
      considered   focus
          1 --- 2 --- 3 --- 4 --- 5

7. Our approach and plan for leadership development is well defined.
           Not   Well
       defined   defined
          1 --- 2 --- 3 --- 4 --- 5

8. Leaders must be accountable and work well with others.
           Not   Strongly
       enforced   enforced
          1 --- 2 --- 3 --- 4 --- 5

9. Leaders must be willing to learn and determined to be better.
         Not a
        factor   Required
          1 --- 2 --- 3 --- 4 --- 5

10. We have regular leadership training and meetings.
            Not   Consistently
        practiced   maintained
           1 --- 2 --- 3 --- 4 --- 5

                  TOTAL _____

Risk Management Scorecard

1. Strong faith expects rather than ignores risk.

Ignore	Expect
risk	risk

    1 --- 2 --- 3 --- 4 --- 5

2. Bigger projects are accompanied by bigger risk.

Level	Bigger
ignored	responsibility

    1 --- 2 --- 3 --- 4 --- 5

3. We identify potential risks before we start every project.

No	Thorough
identification	identification

    1 --- 2 --- 3 --- 4 --- 5

4. We assess the probability and potential impact of each risk.

No	Thorough
assessment	assessment

    1 --- 2 --- 3 --- 4 --- 5

5. After identification and assessment, we take steps to reduce risks.

Accept	Active
risks	reduction

    1 --- 2 --- 3 --- 4 --- 5

6. When risks cannot be eliminated, we develop plans to respond to risks.

Respond	Diligent
later	planning

    1 --- 2 --- 3 --- 4 --- 5

7. We prioritize and rank risks.

All the	Thorough
same	ranking

    1 --- 2 --- 3 --- 4 --- 5

8. We document our risk management plans.

Not	Fully
documented	documented

    1 --- 2 --- 3 --- 4 --- 5

9. We monitor to identify when risks occur.

Not	Actively
monitored	monitored

    1 --- 2 --- 3 --- 4 --- 5

10. High risk projects are started only with prayerful, spiritual certainty.

Level	Proceed only
ignored	when certain

    1 --- 2 --- 3 --- 4 --- 5

    TOTAL _____

Spiritual Priorities Scorecard

1. My vision for this church is strong and becoming clearer.

             Unsure   Strong vision

   1 --- 2 --- 3 --- 4 --- 5

2. My passion for these people is strong and becoming stronger.

             No passion   Strong passion

   1 --- 2 --- 3 --- 4 --- 5

3. I pray for God's mercy upon this church and this city.

             Disconnected   Praying strongly

   1 --- 2 --- 3 --- 4 --- 5

4. I am determined that this church support and plant other churches.

             Internal focus   Strong determination

   1 --- 2 --- 3 --- 4 --- 5

5. I trust that each church member is "fitly framed" and will do their best.

             Wary of others   Fully trusting

   1 --- 2 --- 3 --- 4 --- 5

6. This church will be driven by a determination to reach the lost.

             Stability first   Evangelistic focus

   1 --- 2 --- 3 --- 4 --- 5

7. I believe this church has what this city needs.

             Have doubts   Confident

   1 --- 2 --- 3 --- 4 --- 5

8. This church will maintain its spiritual commitment.

             Weak commitment   Fully committed

   1 --- 2 --- 3 --- 4 --- 5

9. Spiritual effectiveness must be coupled with anointing and renewal.

             Getting by   Anointing is essential

   1 --- 2 --- 3 --- 4 --- 5

10. Success of this church is ordained and requires perseverance.

              May not survive   We will persevere

    1 --- 2 --- 3 --- 4 --- 5

                    TOTAL _____

Scorecard Summary

Scorecard   **Total score**
1. Spiritual Practical Balance   _____
2. Scope Management   _____
3. Schedule Management   _____
4. Resource Management   _____
5. Risk Management   _____
6. Spiritual Priorities Balance   _____
                      GRAND TOTAL   _____

Grand total   **Overall assessment**
0-59   Very weak
60-119   Weak
120-179   Fair
180-239   Strong
240-300   Very strong

Area needing greatest improvement (lowest score)
_____

Steps for improvement
1. _____
2. _____
3. _____
4. _____
5. _____

APPENDIX 2
Church Planter Program Template

The Church Planter Program Template is in two parts.

APPENDIX 2A is the Church Planter Program Template Example. It is a hypothetical timeline for steps that most church planters should plan in their church planting journey. The timeframe for each activity is notional. You will, undoubtedly, have a different timeframe for some, if not many, of the activities. Also, the example is not a set of mandatory activities for each church planted. Not only will your timeframe vary, but the activities themselves will vary. There may be activities that are not necessary for your church. There likely will be others you feel necessary that are not on this list. The list is provided to give a general idea of the activities, the amount of them, and a typical overall timeframe for planting a church.

APPENDIX 2B is the Church Planter Program Template Worksheet. Each of the activities listed in APPENDIX 2A are also listed in APPENDIX 2B. As was just said, you may not require each of these activities, and may require others. The purpose of this worksheet is for you to tailor your church planting timeline as you see fit. You will select your own timeframe for each activity you require. If you wish, you can also track actual completion to compare to your projected completion. This is a tool to use as it helps you best. You may want to make copies of this appendix, especially APPENDIX 2B, for later use, if your plan undergoes significant changes. Such changes are not uncommon.

APPENDIX 2A
Church Planter Program Template Example

Timeframe (months before launch)

Grp	Activity	36	35	34	33	32	31	30	29	28	27	26	25	24	23	22	21	20	19	18	17	16	15	14	13	12	11	10
Call	Answer call	36																										
Call	Communicate call		35																									
Call	Choose governance type			34																								
Call	Register for new church				33																							
Call	New church registered							30																				
Support	Create friend network						31																					
Support	Create prayer network							30																				
Support	Define fin support plan								29																			
Support	Leave old location									28																		
Support	Move to new location										27																	
Support	Start fin support plan													24														
Vision	Define church mission											26																
Vision	Define church values												25															
Vision	Create long-term plan													24														
Administration	Establish bank accts													24														
Administration	Create teaching plan																21											
Administration	Create marketing plan																	20										
Administration	Define admin tools																		19									
Administration	Create fin mgmt plan																			18								
Administration	Create IT plan																				17							
Administration	Initiate fin mgmt tools																					16						
Administration	Start marketing plan																						15					
Administration	Start IT plan																							14				
Management	Create first-year plan																21											
Management	Start first-year plan																	20										
Management	Create annual plans																					16						
Management	Start annual plans																						15					
Management	Update plans																											

| 3 years before launch | 2 years before launch | 1 year |

APPENDIX 2A
Church Planter Program Template Example

9	8	7	6	5	4	3	2	1	0	-1	-2	-3	-4	-5	-6	-7	-8	-9	-10	-11	-12	-13	-14	-15	-16	-17	-18	-19	-20	-21	-22	-23	-24	-25	-26	-27	-28	-29	-30

Timeframe (months before launch)

before launch | 1 year after launch | 2 years after launch | 3 yrs after launch

APPENDIX 2A
Church Planter Program Template Example

Grp	Activity	Timeframe (months before launch)																										
		36	35	34	33	32	31	30	29	28	27	26	25	24	23	22	21	20	19	18	17	16	15	14	13	12	11	10
Governance	Create church team plan																			18								
	Create leadership dev plan																				17							
	Define delegation model																					16						
	Appoint core team																						15					
	Appoint launch team																							14				
	Appoint temp church staff																								13			
	Start leadership dev trng																									12		
	Enact delegation model																										11	
	Create church bylaws																											
	Define church board																											
	Submit bylaws to state																											
	Create church board																											
	Appoint perm church staff																											
Project management	Develop activity tracker																			18								
	Define performance goals																				17							
	Track activities																					16						
	Measure performance																						15					
	Start activity monitoring																							14				
	Start annual reviews																								13			
	Start quarterly reviews																									12		
	Assess performance impact																										11	
	Take corrective actions																											10
	Assess impact of corrections																											
Formation	Develop launch plan																											
	Execute launch plan																											
	Conduct launch service																											
	Acquire church bldg																											
	Buy church insurance																											
	Register permanent location																											
Operation	Create annual ops plan																											
	Start annual ops plan																											

3 years before launch | 2 years before launch | 1 year

APPENDIX 2A
Church Planter Program Template Example

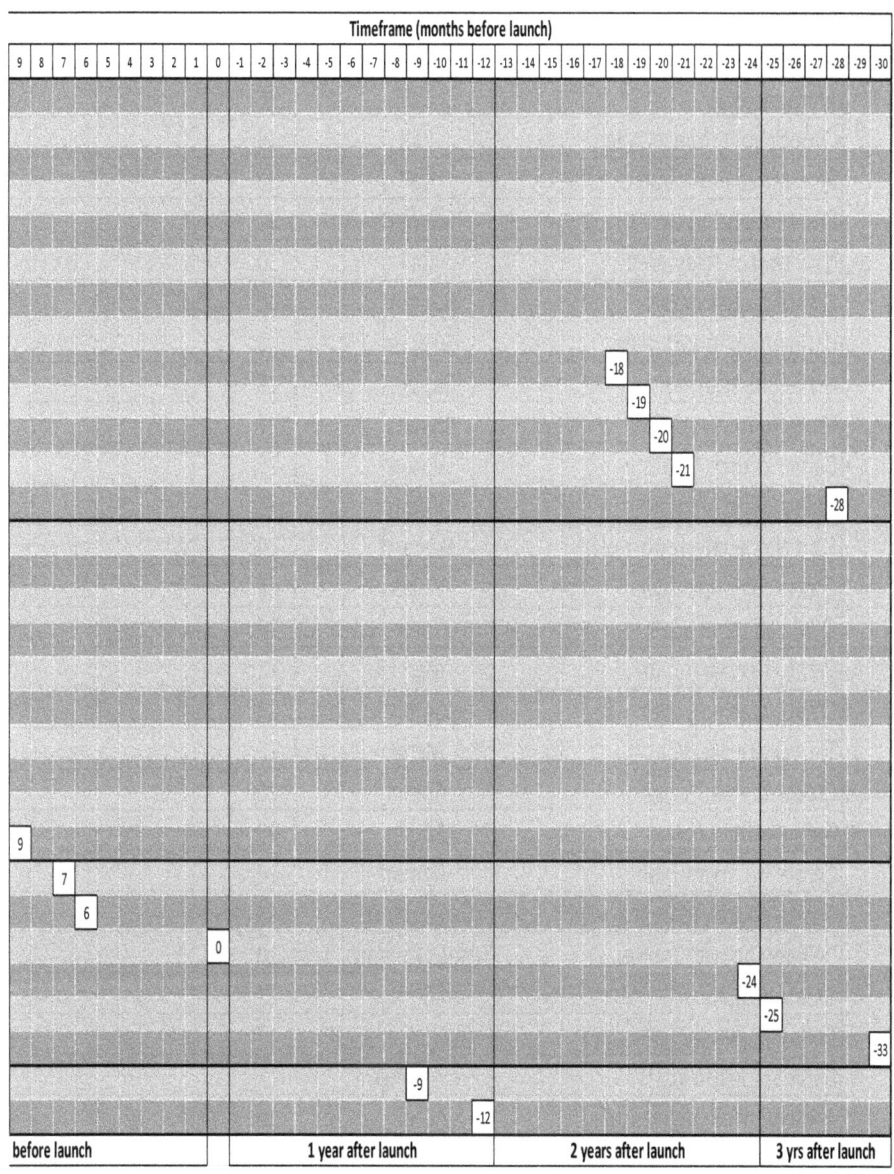

APPENDIX 2B
Church Planter Program Template Worksheet

Activity	Group	Timeframe (months before launch)	Your target date	Date actually completed
Answer call	Call	36		
Announce call	Call	35		
Choose governance type	Call	34		
Register as new church	Call	33		
Create friend network	Support	31		
New church registered	Call	30		
Create prayer network	Support	30		
Define fin support plan	Support	29		
Leave old location	Support	28		
Move to new location	Support	27		
Define church values	Vision	25		
Define church mission	Vision	24		
Start financial support plan	Support	24		
Create long-term plan	Vision	24		
Establish bank accts	Admin	24		
Create first-year plan	Mgmt	21		
Create teaching plan	Admin	21		
Start first-year plan	Mgmt	20		
Create marketing plan	Admin	20		
Define admin tools	Admin	19		
Create fin mgmt plan	Admin	18		
Create church team plan	Governance	18		
Develop activity tracker	Project mgmt	18		
Create IT plan	Admin	17		
Define leadership dev plan	Governance	17		
Define perform goals	Project mgmt	17		
Implement fin mgmt tools	Admin	16		
Create annual plans	Mgmt	16		
Create delegation model	Governance	16		
Track activities	Project mgmt	16		

APPENDIX 2B
Church Planter Program Template Worksheet

Activity	Group	Timeframe (months before launch)	Your target date	Date actually completed
Start marketing plan	Admin	15		
Start annual plans	Mgmt	15		
Appoint core team	Governance	15		
Measure performance	Project mgmt	15		
Start IT plan	Admin	14		
Appoint launch team	Governance	14		
Start activity monitoring	Project mgmt	14		
Appoint temp church staff	Governance	13		
Start annual reviews	Project mgmt	13		
Start leadership dev trng	Governance	12		
Start quarterly reviews	Project mgmt	12		
Enact delegation model	Governance	11		
Assess performance impact	Project mgmt	11		
Take corrective actions	Project mgmt	10		
Assess impact of corrections	Project mgmt	9		
Develop launch plan	Formation	7		
Execute launch plan	Formation	6		
Conduct launch service	Formation	0		
Update plans	Mgmt	-6		
Create annual ops plan	Operation	-9		
Start annual ops plan	Operation	-12		
Create church bylaws	Governance	-18		
Define church board	Governance	-19		
Submit bylaws to state	Governance	-20		
Create church board	Governance	-21		
Acquire church bldg	Formation	-24		
Buy church insurance	Formation	-25		
Appoint perm church staff	Governance	-28		
Register permanent location	Formation	-30		

About the Author

Tim Pruitt is a teacher and project manager with a unique blend of heritage, education and experience. A fourth-generation Pentecostal, he is driven with a passion that the Church can be more effective without sacrificing the vibrancy and demonstration of the Holy Spirit. He has a broad education in science, business and ministry, and has taught in churches of many nations. Tim also managed a project management training program in the aerospace industry. Now "retired", Tim is a Global Educator with the Global Association of Theological Studies, where he has taught in Central and South America, the Caribbean and the Pacific. He has also written *Effective Christianity: Managing Life's Projects*, which serves as a companion to this book, and is described below. He enjoys reading, traveling and playing Sudoku.

Other Books by Timothy C. Pruitt

Effective Christianity: Managing Life's Projects

This book is dedicated to the concept that those who are filled with the Holy Spirit embody that Spirit, and should be the most effective people in the world. Further, we are called to not only be spiritual, but to be effective in accomplishing those things the Spirit leads us to do. By embracing both spiritual conviction and effective management towards His will, we will be more effective in our jobs, homes, churches, and communities, and more effective witnesses.

www.ingramcontent.com/pod-product-compliance
Lightning Source LLC
Chambersburg PA
CBHW060501090426
42735CB00011B/2069